GW00601111

Friendly Word for Windows™ 2.0

Jack Nimersheim

BANTAM BOOKS

NEW YORK · TORONTO · LONDON · SYDNEY · AUCKLAND

Contents

Preface

Most of us become computer users because we have to, because knowledge of a particular software package is needed for a job, or because computer-assisted productivity is essential to success in business. There are hundreds of reasons. Computers and software are only the means to an end. They have become a necessity of life, and this requirement shapes the way we go about learning how to use software.

Not everyone is interested in every detail of a particular program. Here is a quick, no-nonsense introduction that teaches the basic skills needed to use the software.

In approximately 200 pages, each Friendly Computer Book covers the basic features of a specific popular software in a way that will get new users up and running quickly. The result is a series of computer books that has these unifying characteristics:

- **Topic-oriented organization.** Short, self-contained lessons focus on a particular topic or area that is important in learning to use the software.

When you finish the lesson, you'll have mastered an aspect of the software.

- **Spacious layout.** Large type and a spacious layout make the books easy on the eyes and easy to use.

- **Step-by-step approach.** Numbered lists help you to concentrate on the practical steps needed to get your work done.

- **Numerous screen shots.** Each lesson contains at least two screen shots that show you exactly how your screen should look.

- **Frequent use of icons.** Many eye-catching icons—drawing attention to important aspects of the text and software—are placed throughout the book.

- **Lay-flat binding.** Friendly Computer Books stay open as you work.

- **And finally, a low, low price.**

For many users Friendly Computer Books are all they'll need. For others who want to learn more about the software, we've suggested further readings.

Enjoy the friendly approach of Friendly Computer Books!

Ron Petrusha
Series Editor

PART I

GETTING STARTED WITH WORD FOR WINDOWS

◆ *Lesson* ◆

1

What Is Word for Windows?

In a few pages, you'll learn how to install and begin using Word for Windows. Before getting into the nuts-and-bolts of this extraordinary program, however, it might be a good idea to discuss briefly what Word for Windows is, how it works, and what it will allow you to accomplish.

The Word for Windows Advantage

At its most basic level, Word for Windows is a word processor—that is, a program that can be used to create and edit text. If this were all Word for Windows did, it would not be very impressive. Basic word processors, after all, are a dime a dozen in today's world. You can rest assured, however, that Word for Windows is much more than a basic word processor.

Look at Figure 1.1. It shows the beginning of this lesson as it might appear when being written with a basic (that is, non-Windows) word processor. Pretty boring stuff, isn't it?

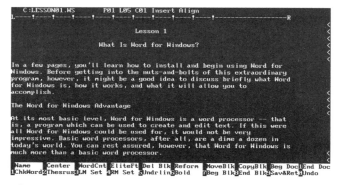

Figure 1.1 A typical word processor

Now feast your eyes on Figure 1.2. This second figure shows the same portion of the current lesson being edited with Word for Windows. Which of these two displays would you rather look at while you work? If you said Figure 1.2, then you're a prime candidate for Word for Windows.

But why do Figures 1.1 and 1.2 look so different from one another? The answer to that question can be found in two places:

- an operating environment known as Windows
- a cryptic computer acronym called WYSIWYG

The Word/Windows Connection

As its name implies, Word for Windows runs under Microsoft's popular Windows operating environment. The Windows graphical user interface, or GUI, makes it easy to use a personal computer.

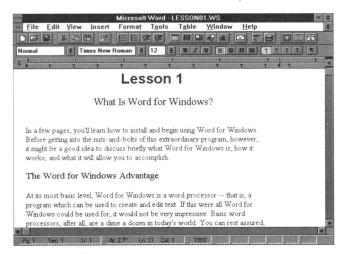

Figure 1.2 Word for Windows at work

 Graphical User Interface, or GUI: A GUI, pronounced "gooey," uses visually oriented, interactive displays to simplify otherwise complicated operations and procedures. Most GUIs, including Windows, let you select text or other data to be affected by an operation and then choose the operation (or operations) from on-screen menus or other display elements.

There are two major advantages associated with working in a GUI like Windows:

1. Windows is designed to provide valuable assistance as you use your PC.
2. All programs that run under Windows use similar techniques to accomplish similar tasks.

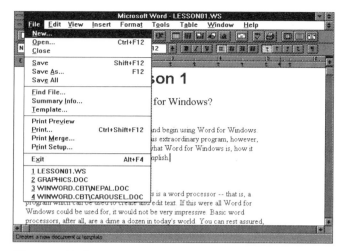

Figure 1.3   The Word for Windows File Menu

Figure 1.3 shows a typical Word for Windows pull-down menu—in this case, the File menu. Selecting an option from this menu is a simple matter of pointing to it with an on-screen pointer and then clicking a mouse button. Compare this with the confusing keyboard commands used by many computer programs and it's easy to see how the highly visual, interactive design of the Windows GUI simplifies mastering even a relatively powerful program like Word for Windows.

Also, the File menu in all Windows applications contains many of the same choices shown in Figure 1.3, including options for loading an already existing file (Open), saving the current file to disk (Save), printing a file (Print), leaving the current application (Exit), and so forth. Consequently, the techniques in this book can be applied to other Windows programs, as well.

The Wonders of WYSIWYG

The second secret to Word for Windows appeal is its reliance on Windows WYSIWYG design. WYSIWYG (pronounced wi-see-wig) stands for what-you-see-is-what-you-get. As you use the various Word for Windows commands to modify the appearance of a document, what you see on your display closely matches how it will look when printed.

Windows WYSIWYG design, combined with Word for Windows ability to incorporate text and graphics into a single file, allows Word for Windows to straddle the fence between standard word processing and desktop publishing. This lets you use Word for Windows to create truly stunning documents like the one shown in Figure 1.4.

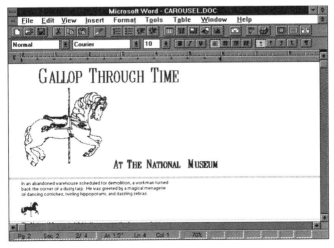

Figure 1.4   Word for Windows straddles the fence between word processing and desktop publishing.

Elegant, Yet Easy

Don't let Word for Windows sheer power intimidate you, however. As I stated earlier, one of the most appealing attributes of Windows (and, by extension, any Windows-based application, including Word for Windows) is the ease with which it allows you to perform even complicated operations. As you'll see throughout the rest of this book, there's nothing magical about Word for Windows. It's simply a well designed program that can be used to create professional looking letters, memos, reports and other, even more complex, documents.

So, let's get started. In the next lesson you'll learn how to install Word for Windows on your PC.

♦ *Lesson* ♦

2

Installing Word for Windows

Before you can use Word for Windows, it has to be installed on your computer. Basically, this involves transferring files from the various Word for Windows distribution diskettes to your hard disk.

Starting Windows

To install Word for Windows, run Setup, the special utility used to install Word for Windows on your system from within a Windows session. To start Windows:

Type **WIN** and press **Enter**.

After a few seconds, Windows displays its Program Manager screen, shown in Figure 2.1. If you already have installed other applications in your Windows environment, obviously, your screen will differ slightly from this figure.

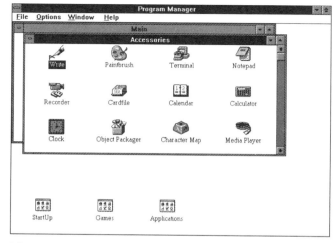

Figure 2.1　The Program Manager display

Look at the two smaller display windows in Figure
2.1 identified as Main and Accessories. These represent
individual program groups that were created when you
initially installed Windows on your computer. As part
of the Word for Windows installation routine, Setup
creates a new program group called, appropriately
enough, Word for Windows.

 Program group: A collection of related programs or data files that occupy a separate display
window within the Program Manager screen. Ar-
ranging files into program groups helps you organize your Windows environment.

Running the Word for Windows Setup Utility

One advantage to working in Windows—and, by extension, applications like Word for Windows—is that it uses the mouse to transform potentially confusing activities into interactive, point-and-click procedures. To see what I mean, use the following steps to display the Program Manager File menu:

1. Move your mouse until the on-screen pointer is pointing to the word "File" on the far left of the Program Manager menu bar.
2. Press and release the left mouse button.

Selecting File displays a pull-down menu listing the various Program Manager File options, as shown in Figure 2.2.

 Point-and-click: Using the mouse to select options within Windows or a Windows application. Basically, this involves moving an on-screen pointer to the desired option (point), then pressing and releasing the left mouse button (click). Point-and-click.

You use the Run option in the pull-down File menu to start the Word for Windows Setup utility.

1. Point to **Run**.
2. Click the left mouse button.

Selecting Run displays the dialog box shown in Figure 2.3. Windows uses dialog boxes to request any addi-

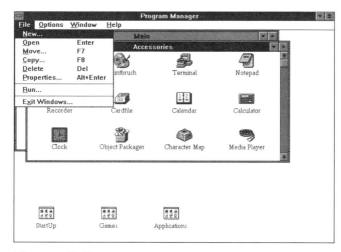

Figure 2.2 The Program Manager File options

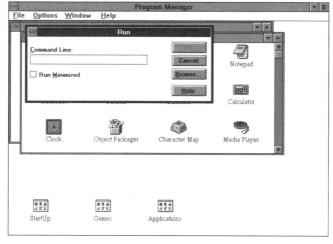

Figure 2.3 The Run dialog box

tional information it requires to complete a selected activity.

To run the Word for Windows Setup utility:

1. Insert the Setup disk—Disk 1 of your Word for Windows distribution diskettes—into the appropriate floppy disk drive. (This can be either drive A or drive B, depending upon whether you're using the 3.5" or 5.25" distribution disks included in the Word for Windows package.)

2. If you're using drive A to install Word for Windows, type **a:setup** and press **Enter**; or if you're using drive B to install Word for Windows, type **b:setup** and press **Enter.**

The first thing Setup does is request some basic information about you, the user. To provide this information:

1. Enter your name and press the **Tab** key.

2. Enter the name of your company or organization. (Enter your name a second time if this is a personal copy of Word for Windows.)

3. Point to **Continue** and click the left mouse button.

4. When Setup asks you to verify the information you have entered, point to **Continue** and click the left mouse button.

Next, Setup asks you to indicate where you want Word for Windows installed; that is, the disk and directory in which it should place the various Word for Windows files. The default location is a directory called **WINWORD**, which Setup will create on drive C, as shown in Figure 2.4. To accept the default location:

Point to **Continue** and click the left mouse button.

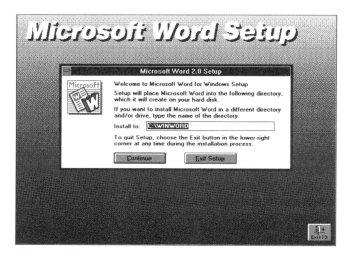

Figure 2.4 Setup lets you specify where it should install Word for Windows.

Tip
Word for Windows requires anywhere from 5Mb to 15Mb of free disk space, depending upon which program options you choose to install. Keep this in mind when you specify a disk drive for your Word for Windows installation.

To pick a new location:

1. Type in a new drive letter and directory.
2. Point to **Continue** and click the left mouse button.

If the specified directory does not already exist, Setup asks you to verify that you want it created. To create the new directory and continue installing Word for Windows:

Point to **Yes** and click the left mouse button.

At this point, Setup lets you select from three types of installation. These include:

- Complete Installation—Installs all Word options and requires approximately 15Mb of disk space. As a first-time user, assuming that your computer has sufficient disk space, you will probably find that this is the best option.
- Custom Installation—Lets you "pick and choose" Word options. The amount of disk space required depends on the options you select.
- Minimum Installation—Installs only the most basic Word options and requires approximately 5.5Mb of disk space.

We're going to choose a Complete Installation, so point to the icon to the left of the **Complete Installation** option and click the left mouse button.

 Icons: Graphical representations of various elements in your Windows environment. These include disk drives, applications, data files, specific commands or procedures, and the like. Clicking on an icon initiates the activity with which that icon is associated.

Next, Setup displays a series of dialog boxes relating to specific activities it should perform during installation. Use the following procedures to create a generic Word for Windows environment:

1. At the WordPerfect dialog box, point to **No** and click the left mouse button. (I'm assuming here that you do not currently use WordPerfect. If you do and want access to help messages that simplify the process of switching over to Word for Windows, choose **Yes** at this prompt.)

2. At the AUTOEXEC.BAT dialog box, point to **Update** and click the left mouse button.

At this point, Setup begins copying the Word for Windows files from the distribution diskettes to your hard disk. When all the files located on a specific distribution disk have been copied, Setup displays a dialog box identifying the next disk it needs. After inserting the requested distribution diskette into the specified disk drive:

1. Point to **OK** and click the left mouse button.

2. When Setup announces that installation is completed, point to **OK** and click the left mouse button.

Tip

As it transfers files to your hard disk, Setup displays a series of messages about Word for Windows. Installation takes approximately 20 minutes, so you'll have plenty of time to read these messages. Go ahead and do so. They provide basic information about some of the Word for Windows features we'll be examining in subsequent lessons.

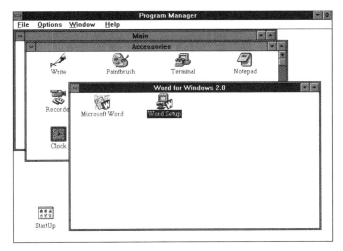

Figure 2.5 Setup creates a Word for Windows program group.

Following installation, your screen will resemble Figure 2.5. As this new screen shows, Setup creates a new program group identified as Word for Windows 2.0 in your Windows display. In the next lesson you'll learn how to use the icons in this program group to start Word for Windows.

Lesson

3

Starting and Exiting Word for Windows

The best way to start learning how to use Word for Windows is by learning how to start Word for Windows; that is, figuring out how to load the program into memory. Like most Windows operations, this is a simple point-and-click procedure.

Starting Word for Windows

The Word for Windows program group created by Setup in the previous lesson contains two icons:

- Microsoft Word
- Word Setup

The latter, Word Setup, can be used to rerun the Setup utility. Specifically, the Word Setup icon is provided so that someone who did not choose Complete Installation in the previous lesson can add extra options—a specific graphics filter, a text conversion utility, and so forth—to his or her Word for Windows environment following initial installation.

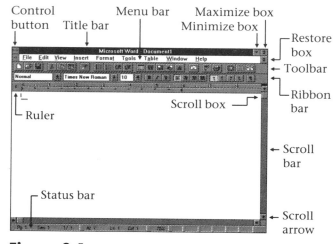

Figure 3.1   The initial Word for Windows display

The Microsoft Word icon, a stylized sheet of paper in the Word for Windows program group window, is the graphical doorway that opens Word for Windows.

To start Word for Windows:

1. Use your mouse to position the mouse pointer over the Microsoft Word icon in the Word for Windows program group.
2. Double-click the left mouse button.

 Double-click: A common procedure used to select certain icons and other items in a Windows display. To double-click on an item, point to the desired item, then quickly press and release the left mouse button twice.

After a few seconds you'll see the opening Word for Windows display. In addition to an initially empty work area that covers most of the screen—the electronic equivalent of a blank piece of paper—the Word for Windows display contains the following elements, identified in Figure 3.1:

Title bar   Shows the name of the current document (**Document1** in Figure 3.1).

Menu bar   Used to access the Word for Windows pull-down option menus.

Toolbar   Provides quick access to a number of commonly used commands, procedures, and program features.

Ribbon bar   Options in this bar allow you to quickly format selected portions of a document.

Ruler   Used to specify margin and tab settings.

Status bar   Used to display useful information about the active document or, alternately, a selected command.

In addition to these elements, which are specific to Word for Windows, Figure 3.1 indicates the following items that are found on all Windows applications:

Control button   Used to display a Control menu that contains options for sizing, moving, shrinking, enlarging, and restoring an application; the Control menu also lets you switch be-

	tween multiple applications running in a Windows session.
Minimize box	Used to reduce a window to an on-screen icon.
Maximize box	Used to enlarge a window to a full-screen display.
Restore box	Used to restore a window to the size it was before you performed a Minimize or Maximize operation on that window.
Scroll box	Windows uses this box to indicate which portion of a document is currently displayed in the window, relative to a file's beginning and end. Dragging this box lets you scroll through the contents of a large file.
Scroll bars	Used to move through a file that's too long or wide to fit in the display window.
Scroll arrows	Used to move through a large file in small increments.

Don't panic if the specific purpose of these objects is not immediately obvious. The goal here is to dip your toes gently into the pool of resources available in Word for Windows, just to see how warm and friendly the waters are. We'll be experimenting with and explaining each of these items in subsequent lessons as we submerge ourselves more completely in the process of creating and editing Word for Windows documents.

The Keyboard Alternative

Obviously, Windows (and, by extension, any Windows application) was designed with the mouse in mind. Because almost any operation you can perform is clearly shown on the Windows display, it's a simple matter to select a given operation using the two-step point-and-click procedure common to mouse operations:

1. Use the mouse to point to the desired item.
2. Click the left mouse button to select this item.

There are times, however, when it's actually easier to use your keyboard to enter a Windows command. This is especially true if you're using a word processor like Word for Windows, where you'll spend much of your time entering text from the keyboard. The availability of keyboard-based alternatives to mouse procedures also helps laptop and notebook owners, who must often use their PCs without the benefit of a mouse.

You'll notice, for example, that each option within the Word for Windows Menu bar contains an underlined letter. (This letter, called a hot key, displays the corresponding pull-down menu when pressed along with the Alt key.) To see how this works, lets select the Tools menu using the appropriate keyboard command:

1. Hold down the **Alt** key.
2. Press **O**.
3. Release the **Alt** and **O** keys.

Your display should now resemble Figure 3.2, which shows the Word for Windows pull-down Tools menu.

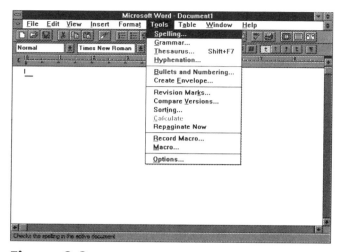

Figure 3.2 You can use keyboard commands to select items from the Menu bar.

Notice that one letter in each of the options contained in this menu also is underlined, indicating its corresponding keyboard command. Unlike selecting a Menu bar option, you don't have to use the Alt key to specify individual items on a pull-down menu.

To remove the Tools menu and return to the Word for Windows workspace:

Press **Esc**.

Although we'll be using mouse commands in the majority of exercises throughout this book, be aware that there are keyboard alternatives available for almost all Word for Windows operations.

Exiting Word for Windows

Equally important as knowing how to start a Windows application is knowing how to exit it and return to the Windows Program Manager. To end the current Word for Windows session:

Click on the **Control** button located at the far left of the Title bar,

or

press **Alt+Spacebar**, if you're using the keyboard.

This displays the Control menu shown in Figure 3.3. Use the Close option to end the current Word for

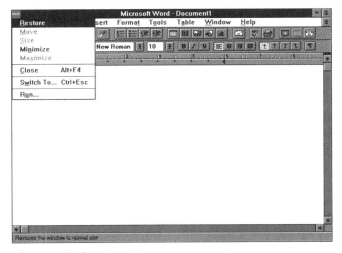

Figure 3.3   The Close command is located in the Control menu.

Windows session and return to Program Manager. Notice that the key sequence **Alt+F4** appears next to the Close option. This is another example of how Windows indicates that a keyboard alternative is available for a specific menu option.

To close Word for Windows:

Click on the **Close** option,

or

press **C** to select Close.

 Tip
Windows uses the plus sign (+) to indicate a multiple-key command sequence. In the above example, therefore, you could have exited Word for Windows by holding down the Alt key and then pressing the F4 function key.

Selecting the Close option ends the current Word for Windows session and returns you to the Windows Program Manager display. But we'll be dipping right back into Word for Windows in the next lesson. That's when you'll begin creating the document we'll use throughout the remainder of this book.

4

Creating a Document

Enough analyzing of Word for Windows. It's time to begin entering and editing text with Word, text that will form a foundation on which we'll build a fairly complex document throughout the remainder of this book. Before getting started, you may need to load Word for Windows from the Program Manager display, which is where we left things at the end of Lesson 3. To start Word for Windows:

Double-click on the **Microsoft Word** icon.

Entering Text

As mentioned in the previous lesson, the initial Word for Windows display resembles a blank piece of paper. From this perspective, beginning a Word for Windows document is not unlike using a traditional typewriter. To start things rolling, let's go ahead and type some text into Word for Windows.

For this exercise, only press the **Enter** key where specifically indicated. As you'll see shortly, Word for

Windows simplifies the writing process, even before you start using some of its more advanced features.

For now, just enter the following passage exactly as it appears here, including any obvious errors it contains:

1. Type **Memo**
2. Press **Enter** twice.
3. Type **To: All Emplloyees**
4. Press **Enter**.
5. Type **From: Personnel**
6. Press **Enter**.
7. Type **Re: Vacation schedules**
8. Press **Enter**.
9. Type **Date: May 11, 1993**
10. Press **Enter** twice.
11. Type **With summer aproaching, it's time to begin planning vacation schedule. As in past years, we hope to limit the degree to which planned vacations disrupt a given dept. We request, therefore, that all dept heads befin coordinating the vacation schedules for thier individual employees soon.**
12. Press **Enter** twice.
13. Type **Please inform this dept of yoor employee's plans as soon as possible.**
14. Press **Enter** twice.
15. Type **Thank you for your corporation in this matter.**
16. Press **Enter**.

When you've finished, your screen should resemble Figure 4.1. Even at this early stage, a quick analysis of this figure reveals one major advantage a word proces-

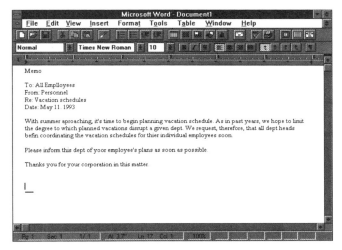

Figure 4.1 A sample document

sor like Word for Windows has over traditional writing methods. Notice that Word for Windows automatically started new lines within the body of the long paragraph, where appropriate. This feature, called *word wrap*, differs from using a typewriter, which forces you to enter carriage returns manually at the end of each line.

Notice also that the status line now reveals some very useful information about your new document. In essence, it provides a "roadmap," of sorts. Specifically, the status line lists:

- which page of a document you're currently on (**Pg 1**);
- how many sections the document contains (**Sec 1**);

- the total number of pages from the beginning of the document followed by the total number of pages it contains (**1/1**);
- the current position of the cursor, also called the insertion point, measured from the top of the page (**At 3.7"**);
- the current line number (**Ln 17**);
- the current column number (**Col 1**);
- the level of magnification at which the current document is being displayed (**100%**).

Next let's examine some additional benefits associated with creating and editing a document using Word for Windows.

Insert vs. Overstrike Mode

Like most word processors, Word for Windows lets you enter text in one of two modes:

- Insert mode, where new text is inserted at the current location, adjusting the position of subsequent text accordingly.
- Overstrike mode, where any new text you enter replaces previously entered text.

By default, Word for Windows uses Insert mode. To see how this works:

1. Position the mouse cursor, which is a stylized "I" beam, between the words "summer" and "approaching" in the first sentence of the document.

2. Click the left mouse button to position the cursor (the insertion point) at the new location.

3. Type **quickly** and press the **Spacebar**.

As you entered the new word, Word for Windows automatically pushed all subsequent text further down in the document. Now try the following:

1. Position the mouse cursor immediately before "yoor" in the second paragraph of the document.
2. Click the left mouse button to position the insertion point at the new location.
3. Press the **Ins** key. (OVR appears in the status bar, indicating that you are now in Overstrike mode.)
4. Type **your**.

This time, your new text replaces the old, allowing you to easily correct the previous misspelling. (Don't worry about any other misspelled words in the memo. In Lesson 17, we'll see how Word for Windows lets you automatically check an entire document to correct misspellings.)

Delete vs. Backspace

Word for Windows provides two ways to remove individual single characters from a document:

*   The **Del** key can be used to remove characters to the right of the current cursor location.
*   The **Backspace** key can be used to remove characters to the left of the current cursor location.

To see how these keys work, try the two exercises that follow. First:

1. Position the mouse cursor immediately after "schedules" in the "Re:" line of the document header.

2. Click the left mouse button to position the insertion point at the new location.
3. Press the **Backspace** key to remove the "s" from "schedules."

Second:

1. Position the mouse cursor immediately before the first "l" in "Emplloyees" in the "To:" line of the document header.
2. Click the left mouse button to position the insertion point at the new location.
3. Press the **Del** key to remove the first "l" from "Emplloyees."

As these two examples demonstrate, the **Del** and **Backspace** keys provide a convenient method for eliminating minor errors in your documents.

Now try to make the following changes to the current original document, using the Insert and Overstrike modes, along with the Insert and Delete keys, where appropriate.

1. Insert the word **our** between "planning" and "vacation" in the first sentence.
2. Replace "planned" in the second sentence with **these**.

When you've finished, your screen should resemble Figure 4.2, which shows the edited document reflecting all of the modifications we've made to this point.

Your Electronic Assistant

We've barely scratched the surface regarding what Word for Windows allows you to do when entering

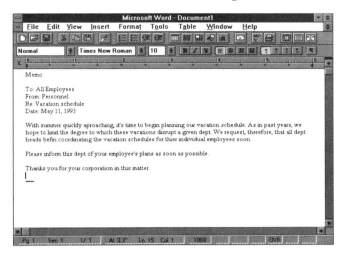

Figure 4.2 Sample document after some editing

and editing text in a document; there's still much more to learn. Before moving on, however, let's take a short break. Use the following commands to exit Word for Windows:

1. Click on the **Control** button located at the far left of the Title bar, or press **Alt+Spacebar**, if you're using keyboard commands.
2. When the Control menu appears, click on the **Close** option, or press **C** to select Close.

Whenever you exit Word for Windows, the program checks to see whether any modifications have been made to the current file since the last time it was saved. If changes have been made, Word for Windows displays the prompt box shown in Figure 4.3, asking whether the revised version of the file should be saved

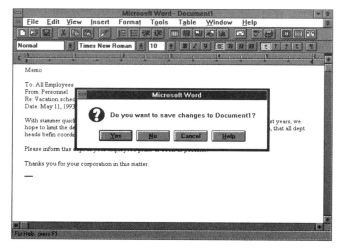

Figure 4.3 Windows prompts you to save changes.

to disk. (This box appears now because we have never saved our test document. In Lesson 10, you'll learn how to save a document manually, using the File menu.) In essence, Word for Windows functions like an electronic assistant, preventing you from inadvertently losing work by prematurely ending an editing session.

To save the current document:

Click on **Yes** in the prompt box.

Word for Windows displays the Save As dialog box, shown in Figure 4.4, asking you to assign a name to the current document. We'll examine how to use this dialog box more extensively in Lesson 10. For now:

1. Type **initial.doc** and press **Enter**.
2. When the Summary Info dialog box appears (which we'll also examine more extensively in Lesson 10), press **Enter** a second time.

This saves the work we've done until now and ends the current editing session. As noted earlier, however, we still have many Word for Windows features to examine. In the next lesson, we'll build upon this initial work and see how Word for Windows handles even longer documents.

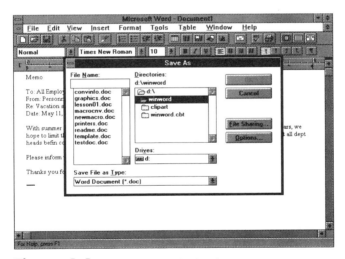

Figure 4.4   The Save As dialog box

◆ *Lesson* ◆

5

Working with Longer Documents

We're going to jump right back into Word for Windows and expand the short memo created in the previous lesson. Doing so will allow us to examine how Word for Windows handles documents larger than a single display screen. As you did at the beginning of the previous chapter, load Word for Windows from the Program Manager display by double-clicking on the **Microsoft Word** icon.

Opening a Document

First we'll need to retrieve that portion of the memo that already exists. This requires using the Open option on the Word for Windows File menu.

1. Click on **File** in the Word for Windows Menu bar.
2. Click on the **Open** option.

This displays the **Open** dialog box shown in Figure 5.1. Notice that the file listing on the left-hand side of this

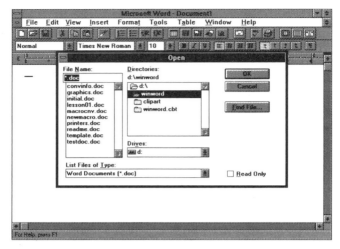

Figure 5.1   The Open dialog box

dialog box contains a file called **initial.doc**, the name
we assigned to our memo at the end of the previous
lesson. To load this file:

Double-click on **initial.doc** in the **Open** dialog
box.

This loads the selected file. The Title bar on your Word
for Windows display now contains the name of this
file, rather than the generic **DOCUMENT1** it held in
the previous exercises. Let's increase the size of our
memo by entering some additional text.

1. Position the mouse cursor immediately after
"possible" at the end of the second paragraph.

2. Click the left mouse button to position the in-sertion point at the new location.
3. Press **Del** to remove the period.
4. Type **, using the following form:**
5. Press **Enter** twice.
6. Type **Department:**
7. Press **Enter** twice.
8. Type **Employee's Name:**
9. Press **Enter** twice.
10. Type **Position Title:**
11. Press **Enter** twice.
12. Type **Total Vacation Days:**
13. Press **Enter** twice.
14. Type **Return Date:**
15. Press **Enter** twice.

When you've finished the previous sequence, your screen should resemble Figure 5.2. Notice that as you entered these additional lines, the first portion of the initial memo scrolled off the top of the display window. With this new text, we can begin exploring the Word for Windows features to manage large documents.

Scrolling a Large Document

One way to recall text that has scrolled off the display window is with the scroll arrows. Our memo is now too long (as opposed to too wide) to fit into a single display window; therefore, use the scroll arrow at the top of the vertical scroll bar the beginning of the memo. Click on the arrow at the top of the vertical scroll bar until the top portion of the document is visible.

Figure 5.2 Word for Windows automatically scrolls portions of a large document off the display window.

You can also drag the scroll button to move through a large document:

1. Point to the vertical scroll button.
2. Drag this button approximately halfway down the vertical scroll bar.
3. Release the left mouse button.

This returns the bottom portion of the memo to the display window.

 Drag: A common procedure used to move items in a Windows display. To drag an item, point to it and hold down the left mouse button while you move it to the desired location.

Working with Multiple Windows

A second way to manage a large document is to place different sections of it in separate windows. This allows you to work with discrete portions of the file in each open window. To split our sample memo into two separate windows:

1. Click on the **Window** option in the Word for Windows Menu bar.
2. Select **New** from the pull-down Window menu.

Word for Windows opens a second document window for the current file. In this example, the new window contains the first part of the memo. You can identify the new window, which automatically becomes the active window, by the fact that its Title bar contains the name **INITIAL.DOC:2**.

Of course, to coordinate activities between these two windows, you must be able to access both of them. The easiest way to do this is by splitting your display. Let's go ahead and do this.

1. Click on the **Window** option in the Word for Windows Menu bar.
2. Select **Arrange All** from the pull-down Window menu.

Your screen should now resemble Figure 5.3, which shows the Word for Windows display split between two windows, each holding a separate portion of our sample memo.

Only one display window can be active at any given time, which Windows identifies by highlighting its Title bar. The actual color used for highlighting depends on which color scheme you chose when install-

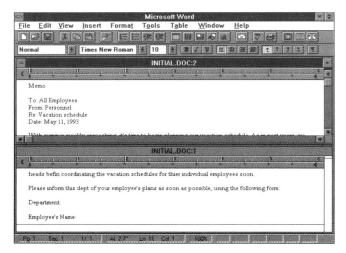

Figure 5.3 Splitting the display lets you place portions of a large document in separate windows.

ing Windows on your system. INITIAL.DOC:2 is currently the active window. Now try the following:

1. Click on the Title bar for **INITIAL.DOC:1**. This makes it the active window.
2. Drag the scroll button in the INITIAL.DOC:1 window to the top of the vertical scroll bar. Notice that only the contents of the active window are scrolled.
3. Use the mouse to position the insertion point after "Personnel" in the "From:" line of in the INITIAL.DOC:1 window and click the left mouse button.
4. Press the **Spacebar** and type **Department**. Notice that this latest modification to our sam-

ple memo is automatically reflected in both windows.

5. Click on the **Maximize** button, the triangle pointing toward the top of the screen on the far right of the INITIAL.DOC:1 Title bar. This enlarges the INITIAL.DOC1 window to fill the entire screen.

6. Click on the **Restore** button, the two triangles on the far right of the Word for Windows Menu bar. This returns the INITIAL.DOC:1 window to its previous size and location, restoring the split-screen display.

7. Click on the Title bar for **INITIAL.DOC:2** to make this the active window.

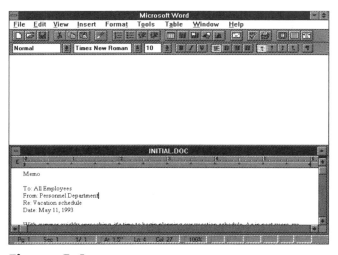

Figure 5.4   It's easy to open and close multiple display windows.

8. Click on the **Control** button for this window, the box on the far left of the INITIAL.DOC:2 Title bar. This displays the Control menu for the INITIAL.DOC2 display window.

9. Click on **Close**. Your screen should now resemble Figure 5.4, which shows a single INITIAL.DOC window occupying the bottom half of the display.

10. Click on the **Maximize** button on the far right of the INITIAL.DOC Title bar. This returns INITIAL.DOC to a full-screen display window.

The exercises in this lesson were designed to help you feel comfortable navigating the Word for Windows display. In truth, we didn't do much but open, resize, and reorganize display windows. The procedures learned in this lesson will come into play during subsequent lessons, however, as we begin polishing the appearance and contents of our sample memo.

6

Working with Word for Windows Menus

As inevitably happens in a book like this, we've already had to use certain Word for Windows features before we could fully explain them. In this lesson we'll look more closely at the various Word for Windows menus, some of which you've already encountered. In the process, we'll examine how these menus are organized, and the types of activities each allows you to perform.

Menu Magic

The Word for Windows pull-down menus provide a convenient way to initiate almost any activity you'll need to perform as you create and refine your documents. Some of the operations available through the various Word for Windows menus are universal to all Windows applications; others are unique to Word for Windows, based on functions used primarily for word processing and document formatting.

As a rule, similar types of activities are grouped together in a single pull-down menu. The following pull-down menus are available from the Word for Windows Menu bar:

File

This menu contains options relating to managing your documents and, in some cases, the individual files they contain. It is used to create, open, close, save, and organize your disk files. The File menu also contains several menu options used to prepare a document for printing.

Edit

This menu contains options used to edit or otherwise modify the contents of a document. Common word processing procedures initiated from the Edit menu include cut-and-paste and find-and-replace. The Edit menu also contains several options that let you create links between your Word for Windows documents and items created with other Windows applications.

View

This menu is used to change the appearance and contents of your Word for Windows display. You can, for example, turn the Tool bar, Ribbon and Ruler on or off. The View menu also includes options that allow you to create headers, footers, footnotes and other annotations for a document.

Insert   This menu is used to insert a variety of items quickly at a specified location within a document. These include page breaks, date and time stamps, index entries, graphic images, the contents of other files, and the like.

Format   This menu contains most of the options relating to the desktop publishing capabilities of Word for Windows; that is, taking text and turning it into an attractive, professional looking printed document. Values set from this menu include character fonts and type sizes, special text characteristics (boldface, underlining, italics, etc.), justification, page margins, line spacing, and the like.

Tools   This menu provides access to several utilities included with Word for Windows that help you write more effectively; for example, the spelling checker, thesaurus, grammar checker, and hyphenation rules. This menu also includes several options for analyzing the progress of a document through multiple revisions. A special Macro tool can be used to automate frequently performed operations.

Table   This menu contains the options used to create and refine the appearance of tabular information included in a document.

Window   This menu is invoked to open, ar-
                 range, and switch between multiple
                 windows in a Word for Windows ses-
                 sion.

Help   This menu is used to request addi-
                 tional information about specific
                 Word for Windows features and func-
                 tions.

Again, don't panic if you don't yet understand all of
the options and activities listed on a specific menu.
We'll be examining most of them in hands-on exercises throughout the remainder of this book. In fact,
you've already encountered and used some of them—
the Window options, for example, which you used in
the previous lesson.

In this lesson, we're going to concentrate on learning how to access the various Word for Windows
menus, using either the mouse or the appropriate keyboard command. We'll also explain the meaning of the
symbols and notations found on some menus.

Displaying a Menu

We've touched on this already, but let's review it here.
There are two ways to display a Word for Windows
pull-down menu:

1. Use your mouse to position the mouse pointer
   over the desired menu listing in the Word for
   Windows Menu bar and click the left mouse button.
2. Hold down the **Alt** key and press the underlined
   letter in the name of the menu you want to
   display.

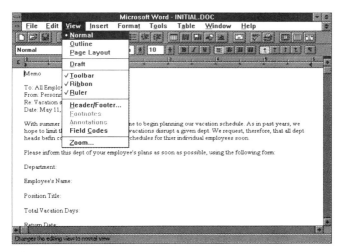

Figure 6.1 The View menu

For example, to access the View menu:

Click on **View** in the Word for Windows Menu bar,

or

press **Alt+V**.

This displays the View menu, shown in Figure 6.1.

Selecting Menu Options

Once a pull-down menu is displayed, you can select an option it contains in one of three ways:

1. Click on the desired menu option.
2. Press the underlined letter on the desired option.
3. Use the arrow keys to highlight the desired option and press **Enter**.

For example, to remove the Ruler from your Word for Windows display:

Click on **Ruler** in the View menu,

or

press **R**,

or

use the **down arrow** key to highlight the **Ruler** option, then press **Enter**.

Your screen should now resemble Figure 6.2, which shows the Word for Windows display with the on-screen Ruler turned off.

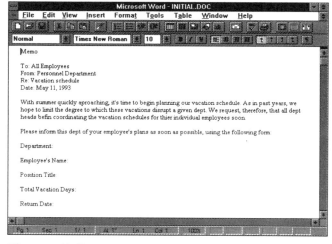

Figure 6.2   After turning off the ruler

Special Menu Notations

Word for Windows uses special notations to indicate additional information about items that appear on its pull-down menus. To see these, let's redisplay the View menu:

Click on **View** in the Word for Windows Menu bar,

or

press **Alt+V**.

CHECK MARKS

Compare your current display with Figure 6.1. Notice that unlike the earlier figure, your screen does not show a check mark to the left of the Ruler option. Word for Windows uses check marks to indicate when a toggled option—a menu option than can be either turned on or off—is active. When you turned off the on-screen Ruler in the previous exercise, Word for Windows removed the check mark from the corresponding menu option.

DOTS

Next look at the three options located at the top of the View menu: **Normal**, **Outline**, and **Page Layout**. Only one of these options, which you use to specify how you want text to be displayed on your screen, can be active at any given time. The dot to the left of Normal option indicates that it is currently active.

ELLIPSES

Two options on the View menu, **Header/Footer** and **Zoom**, are followed by a series of three periods, or ellipses (**...**). Some activities require additional steps that cannot be performed by selecting a single menu option. Word for Windows uses this symbol to indicate that selecting one of these menu options does not immediately perform an activity, but instead advances you to a second menu or, in many cases, a dialog box. We'll discuss how to use dialog boxes in the next lesson.

UNAVAILABLE OPTIONS

Notice that two options on the View menu, **Footnotes** and **Annotations**, are displayed in light gray, rather than black, letters. Word for Windows uses this lighter highlight to indicate menu options that are currently unavailable. Generally, this is because you must perform some other activity before they can be used to accomplish anything. For example, a footnote must already exist in our sample memo before you can select it using the Footnote option.

KEYBOARD SHORTCUTS

To demonstrate the final notation that appears on the Word for Windows pull-down menus, you need to display the Edit menu.

Click on **Edit** in the Word for Windows Menu bar,

or

press **Alt+E**,

or,

with the View menu already displayed, press the **left arrow** key.

That last procedure was thrown at you without warning. Consider it a pleasant surprise. This is another example of a keyboard command you can use in place of your mouse. Once one pull-down menu is displayed, the left and right arrow keys allow you to access the other pull-down menus.

Your screen should now resemble Figure 6.3, which shows the Word for Windows Edit menu. Notice that specific keys or key combinations are listed to the right of selected options within this menu. The **Copy** option, for example, is followed by the key combination

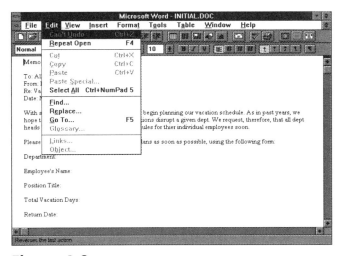

Figure 6.3 Word for Windows indicates when a keyboard shortcut is available for a menu option.

Ctrl+C. Word for Windows uses this technique to indicate when a keyboard shortcut is available to perform a frequently used operation. Many times, especially when entering text into a Word for Windows document, it's more convenient to use a shortcut, rather than take your fingers off the keyboard and rely on pull-down menus.

Removing a Menu

Should you ever display a menu and then decide not to use any of its options, Word for Windows provides an easy method for removing that menu without initiating any actions. To do this:

Press the **Esc** (Escape) key.

Pressing Esc once removes the currently displayed menu and leaves the Menu bar active. (Notice on your display, for example, that Edit is still highlighted, even though the Edit menu is gone.) At this point, you could use the arrow keys to select another Menu bar item and then press Enter to display the corresponding pull-down menu. To deactivate the Menu bar entirely and continue editing your document:

Press **Esc** a second time.

As you can see, the Word for Windows pull-down menus provide quick and easy access to a wide range of commands, activities, and operations. As stated earlier, specific information on how to use the various menu options will be presented in subsequent lessons as we polish our sample memo. In the next lesson, we'll take a look at how you use the dialog boxes associated with some menu options.

Working with Dialog Boxes

As mentioned in the previous lesson, some Word for Windows operations are too complex to complete by selecting a single menu option. Generally, this is because the program needs additional information about whatever activity you want to perform.

This should not be perceived as a weakness in Word for Windows. It isn't a program, like so many computer programs, that requires too much work from the user to accomplish something. Rather, it indicates how powerful Word for Windows is. Best of all, Word for Windows uses a special feature of the Windows environment—dialog boxes—to transform even complicated operations into easy, point-and-click procedures.

What Is a Dialog Box?

In the *Word for Windows User's Guide*, Microsoft gives the following definition for a dialog box: "A window that appears temporarily to request information."

That's pretty bland, in my opinion. A more apropos definition of a dialog box would be the following: "A window containing a series of specific instructions, options, or prompts that allow even inexperienced users to perform complex and potentially confusing activities." That captures much more adroitly—again, in my opinion—how powerful and useful a tool a dialog box can be.

But why attempt to describe a dialog box when it's easier to show you what I mean. To do this, let's take a second look at the **Save As** dialog box, which we encountered in Lesson 4.

1. Click on **File** in the Word for Windows Menu bar.
2. Click on the **Save As** option.

The Save As operation provides a good example of how to use a dialog box. It contains several items that demonstrate how the various objects in a dialog box work. These include:

- command buttons
- text boxes
- list boxes
- drop-down list boxes
- option buttons
- check boxes

The Save As dialog box contains specific examples of the first four items on this list.

Selecting the Save As option displays the dialog box shown in Figure 7.1. During a Word for Windows session, you would use this dialog box to assign a new name to the current version of your document and save it to disk.

Using Command Buttons

Command buttons are simply on-screen buttons that, when selected, carry out or cancel a command. Figure 7.1 contains four command buttons, which are marked **OK**, **Cancel**, **File Sharing**, and **Options**. Clicking on a command button initiates the corresponding activity.

In some cases, selecting a command button advances you to additional options. Should this be the case, the command button includes ellipses (**...**), just like multi-level menu options. The **File Sharing** and **Options** buttons in Figure 7.1 are examples of command buttons that, when selected, call up additional dialog boxes. We'll see how command buttons work in a few paragraphs, when we close the Save As dialog box.

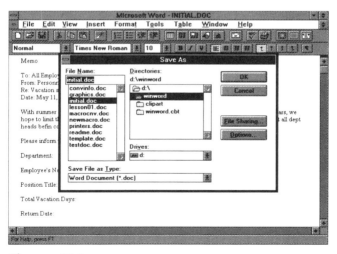

Figure 7.1 Dialog boxes request any additional information required to complete a specific operation.

Using Text Boxes

Text boxes are fields into which you type specific information, using the keyboard. The **File Name** box in Figure 7.1 is an example of a text box. Notice that this box currently contains the default name of our sample memo, **initial.doc**. The text box provides a way to assign a totally new name to the current document, if you want to. To see how a text box works, let's go ahead and do this.

1. Position the mouse pointer immediately to the left of the "i" in "initial.doc."
2. Click the left mouse button.
3. Use the **Del** key to remove the word "initial" from the current name.
4. Type **mymemo**.

As this example demonstrates, the standard editing commands described in Lesson 4 (**Backspace** and **Del**) are available when entering text into a text box.

Using List Boxes

List boxes provide you with a list of choices from which you select the one you want. Figure 7.1 contains two list boxes. The one directly under the **File Name** text box contains a listing of files already in the current directory. Immediately to the left of this is a second list box you can use to move to different directories on the active hard disk.

If a list box contains more options than will fit in a single window, a scroll bar is displayed, which enables you to move up and down the list. To select an option from a list box, simply find and then double-click on the desired item.

To move to the root directory of the current drive:

Double-click on **c:** immediately above **winword** in the directory list box.

To return to the winword directory:

Double-click on **winword**.

Using Drop-Down List Boxes

A drop-down list box initially displays a single selection, but provides easy access to more options. Drop-down list boxes are identified by a down arrow located to the right of the current selection. Figure 7.1 contains two drop-down list boxes marked **Drives** and **Save File as Type**. Selecting the arrow displays the additional options available for a drop-down list box.

To change the active drive:

Click on the down arrow to the right of **c:** in the **Drives** box.

A box appears listing all the available drives on your system, as illustrated in Figure 7.2. Clicking on a different letter would make the corresponding drive the active disk drive.

CLOSING AN OPTION BOX

Unfortunately, the **Save As** dialog box doesn't contain examples of the two remaining dialog box tools. So, let's close it. In fact, let's use the Cancel button to close it without implementing any of the changes we've made.

Click on the **Cancel** command button.

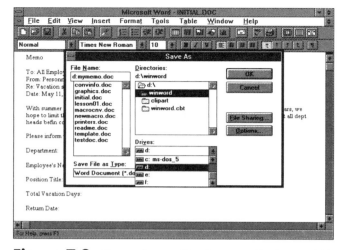

Figure 7.2 Drop-down list boxes display additional options.

This closes the **Save As** dialog box and returns you to the Word for Windows workspace.

Check and Option Boxes

Next we'll open a dialog box containing the two items we've not yet seen.

1. Click on **Edit** in the Word for Windows Menu bar.
2. Click on the **Find** option.

Selecting the Find option displays the dialog box shown in Figure 7.3. In addition to command buttons and a text box, this dialog box contains examples of check and option boxes.

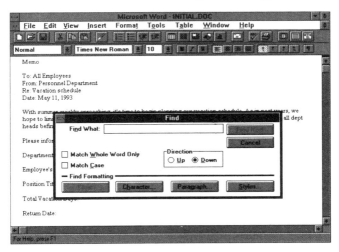

Figure 7.3 Some dialog boxes contain option boxes and check boxes.

To use a check box in this dialog box:

1. Type **Return Date** in the **Find What** text box.
2. Click on the square check box to the left of **Match Case**.
3. Click on the **Find Next** command box.

Word for Windows finds and highlights the specified text, as shown in Figure 7.4. As the previous exercise illustrates, you use a check box to turn on or off an option. In this example, we told Word for Windows to match exactly, including case, the text entered in the **Find What** text box.

Option boxes represent mutually exclusive options. The Find option box, for example, contains option boxes to specify whether you want to scan a document

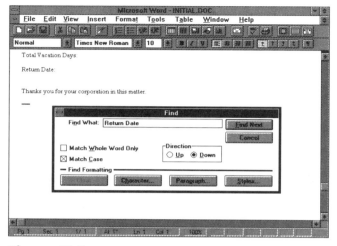

Figure 7.4   Use check boxes to turn options on and off.

Up or **Down**—from the current insertion point to the beginning of the document or to the end of the document, respectively. You can't do both of these. Hence, the phrase in my earlier description, "mutually exclusive."

Let's see how an option button works.

1. Position the mouse pointer immediately to the left of the "R" of "Return Date" in the **Find What** text box.
2. Click the left mouse button.
3. Use the **Del** key to remove the current text in this text box.
4. Type **memo**.
5. Click on the square check box to the left of **Match Case**.

6. Click on the option box to the left of **Up**.

7. Click on the **Find Next** command box.

We accomplished two things in this exercise: First, we turned off the Match Case box. This told Word for Windows to find the specified text, regardless of whether it was written in uppercase letters, lowercase letters, or a combination of the two. Second, we told Word for Windows to search starting from the previous find to the beginning of the document.

Consequently, Word for Windows returned us to the beginning of the document, where it found **Memo**.

Now that we've seen how check and option boxes work, let's exit the **Find** dialog box and move on.

Click on the **Cancel** command button.

You'll encounter dialog boxes throughout the remainder of this book. The information in this lesson should help you to use them well and wisely.

◆ *Lesson* ◆

8
The Word for Windows Toolbar

If you think pull-down menus are convenient to use, wait until you see the Word for Windows Toolbar in action. It transforms many commonly used commands and procedures into single, point-and-click operations.

The Toolbar Options

Figure 8.1 shows the Word for Windows Toolbar. It is the horizontal line of command buttons immediately below the Menu bar. Reading from left to right, the individual buttons in the Toolbar provide immediate access to the following operations:

New	Opens a new document.
Open	Loads an already existing document.
Save	Saves the current document, using its default name.
Cut	Removes selected text or graphics and places them in the Windows Clipboard.

Figure 8.1   The Word for Windows Toolbar

Copy	Copies selected text or graphics to the Windows Clipboard.
Paste	Inserts text or graphics from the Clipboard at the current cursor location.
Undo	Reverses the last command you executed.
Numbered List	Creates numbered lists from selected paragraphs.
Bulleted List	Creates non-numbered lists in which each item is preceded by a bullet or some other character.
Unindent	Moves selected paragraphs to the previous tab stop.
Indent	Moves selected paragraphs to the next tab stop.
Table	Inserts a table at the current cursor location.
Text Columns	Formats selected text using newspaper-style columns.
Frame	Creates a nonprinting frame into which you can then import text or graphics.
Draw	Starts the Microsoft Draw program from within Word for Windows.
Graph	Starts the Microsoft Graph program from within Word for Windows.

Envelope	Creates an envelope that will be printed with the current document.
Spelling	Starts the Word for Windows spelling checker.
Print	Prints all pages of the active document.
Zoom Whole Page	Displays the current page, in reduced size, to see how it will appear when printed.
Zoom 100%	Displays a document a full size, in normal view. (This is the default Word for Windows display, which we've been using until now.)
Zoom Page Width	Adjusts the display so that the entire width of a document can be seen.

That's over twenty different commands, each immediately accessible from its own command button (some of which, admittedly, you don't yet know how to use). And this just covers the commands included on the Toolbar immediately following installation of Word for Windows. You also can add custom buttons designed to automatically execute your own commands that you use regularly in the course of your work.

 Note: Creating custom Toolbar buttons is an advanced topic, one that's somewhat beyond the scope of this introductory book. For information on how this is done, see Chapter 38 in your *Word for Windows User's Guide*, "Customizing Menus, the Keyboard, and the Toolbar."

Using the Toolbar

As mentioned at the beginning of this lesson, the Word for Windows Toolbar represents the epitome of point-and-click procedures. How easy is the Toolbar to use? Let's find out.

1. Point to the **Save** button, the third button from the left on the Toolbar—a stylized floppy disk icon.
2. Click the left mouse button.

Guess what? You just saved the current version of your document to a disk file under its current name, **initial.doc**. Like I said, the epitome of point-and-click. But that was almost too easy. You didn't really get to see anything happen. So, try this:

1. Point to the **Zoom Whole Page** button, the third button from the right on the Toolbar.
2. Click the left mouse button.

Your screen should now resemble Figure 8.2. This screen provides a representative display of how the current page will look when printed.

To return to the Normal display:

1. Point to the **Zoom 100%** button, the second button from the right on the Toolbar.
2. Click the left mouse button.

This returns the screen to the familiar display we've been using until now to examine Word for Windows.

Selecting Text for Operations

Some Toolbar commands—indeed, as you'll see throughout this book, many Word for Windows oper-

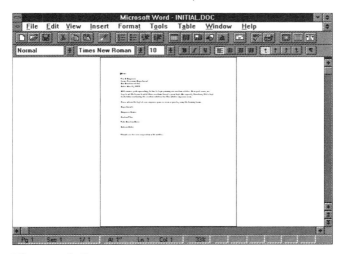

Figure 8.2 A quick click on the Toolbar shows you how a page will look when printed.

ations—require you to select a block of text before they can be executed. To see how this works:

1. Point to the far left of the line that begins **Department:** (The mouse cursor should change to an arrow when you do this).
2. Hold down the left mouse button.
3. Drag the mouse toward you until all lines from **Department:** to **Return Date:** are highlighted.
4. Release the left mouse button.
5. Point to the **Indent** button, the eleventh button from the left on the Toolbar—a stylized block of text with an arrow pointing to the right.
6. Click the left mouse button.

Figure 8.3 Some Word for Windows commands require you to select a block of text prior to execution.

Your screen should now resemble Figure 8.3, in which each line in the selected block of text has been indented, relative to the left-hand margin of our sample memo.

In the previous steps you used the Word for Windows selection bar, an unmarked area running down the left side of the document window. The selection bar provides an easy way to quickly select a block of text. Later lessons will demonstrate additional ways that you can use the selection bar.

Before ending this lesson, save the changes we just made to our document—using the Toolbar shortcut, of course.

1. Point to the **Save** button.
2. Click the left mouse button.

That does it. Now, let's move on.

◆ *Lesson* ◆

9

Getting Help

I've pointed out several times in previous lessons how simple Word for Windows is to use, how "friendly" this program can be. Perhaps the best indication of Word for Windows congeniality is the ease with which it provides assistance to inexperienced users through a comprehensive on-line Help feature. When you're working in Word for Windows, specific instructions for most of its commands are a single keystroke away.

The Help Key

The easiest way to access Word for Windows on-line Help is by pressing the Help key—the F1 function key. What happens when you press F1 depends on what you're doing at the time. To see what I mean:

Press **F1**.

Because you were performing no specific operation when you requested Help, your screen should now resemble Figure 9.1, which shows the Word for Windows Help Index. Using the Help Index is the most

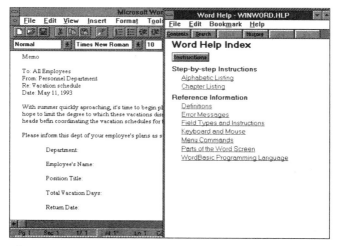

Figure 9.1 The Word for Windows Help Index

"generic" approach to finding help on a specific topic. We'll discuss how the Help Index works in a few paragraphs. For now, however, let's check out another aspect of the Word for Windows Help feature.

First, close the current Help window.

1. Select **File** from the Help menu bar.
2. Select the **Exit** option, which closes Help and returns you to the current document.

Context-Sensitive Help

The Word for Windows Help feature is *context-sensitive.* This means it will, whenever appropriate, display information about the specific operation you are performing at the time. To see what how this works:

1. Press **Alt-V** to display the View menu.
2. Press **F1**.

Word for Windows automatically displays the Help message shown in Figure 9.2. Notice that this message contains information about the Normal option, which was highlighted on the View menu when you pressed F1. If a different menu option had been highlighted at the time, Word for Windows would have displayed a different Help message.

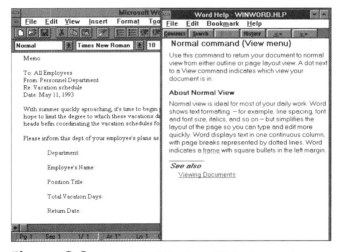

Figure 9.2   Word for Windows Help feature is context-sensitive.

Navigating Help

But what are you supposed to do if you're not certain how to begin an operation you want to perform? That's where the more generic Help options come into play. Navigating Word for Windows Help system is an exercise in simplicity.

Select **Help** from the Word for Windows Menu bar.

This displays the Help menu shown in Figure 9.3. You use the Help menu to request information about virtually any Word for Windows command or procedure, regardless of what you're doing at the time.

The **Getting Started** and **Learning Word** options run on-line tutorials designed to teach you basic

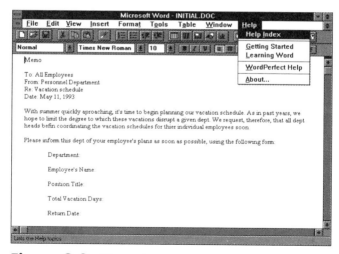

Figure 9.3   The Help Menu

Word for Windows operations. The **WordPerfect Help** option helps current WordPerfect users make the transition to working in the Word for Windows environment. The most flexible way to request assistance from Word for Windows, however, is through its Help Index. To access the Help index:

1. Select **Help Index** from the pull-down Help menu. This displays the Help Index, which you saw in Figure 9.1.
2. Point to **Alphabetic Listing**.
3. Click the left mouse button.

Did you notice that, in Step 1, the mouse arrow changed to a pointing finger? This symbol appears whenever a section on the Help display provides access to additional information about the selected topic. In this case, for example, Help displays an alphabetical listing of topics relating to specific Word for Windows operations, as shown in Figure 9.4. Like almost all Windows displays, this one lets you use a scroll bar, scroll buttons, and arrows to access information not initially shown in the window.

The Help Controls

Notice the control buttons located just below the Help Menu bar in Figure 9.4. They resemble the controls on a cassette recorder or VCR in that you can click them to initiate a specific operation.

- Contents returns you to the Help Index.
- Search lets you request Help on a specific topic.

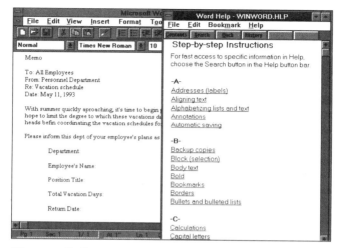

Figure 9.4   Portions of the Help screen provide access to additional information about a topic.

- Back recalls the Help message or menu that appeared immediately before the one currently displayed.
- History displays a prompt box containing a listing of the most recently performed Help operations.
- The reverse button (<<) moves you backward through linked Help messages.
- The forward button (>>) moves you forward through linked Help messages.

Go ahead and experiment with Help. Because it's running in a separate window from Word for Windows, nothing you do will affect our sample memo. I'll wait here until you're finished.

CLOSING HELP

To end an on-line Help session and return to Word for Windows:

1. Select **File** from the Help menu bar.
2. Select the **Exit** option.

As you saw earlier, this ends the current Help session and returns you to the main Word for Windows display.

Using Undo

Before moving on, we're going to look at a helpful Word for Windows feature: Undo. Word for Windows keeps a record of the last edit you've performed. If you then decide to revert to the previous version, you can use the **Undo** option to do so. To see what I mean, try the following;

1. Select **Edit** from the Word for Windows Menu bar.
2. Select the **Undo** option.

The exact wording of the Undo option, and what Undo accomplishes, depends on the last action you took. For example, if you boldfaced a block of text and then wanted to reverse the action, selecting Edit Undo Formatting would accomplish this. The availability of the Undo feature allows you to experiment with a variety of formatting options and quickly recover from any that don't work out quite like you expect.

10

Saving Your Document

Although this lesson covers a procedure we've already seen in action, making sure you know how to save the work you do in Word for Windows is an important enough topic that it deserves its own lesson. There are also additional features associated with the Save command that we've not yet encountered, which will be discussed here.

The Many Faces of Save

Word for Windows provides several ways to save your work. These include:

- the **File/Save** command (**Shift+F12**)
- the **File/Save As** command (**F12**)
- the Toolbar **Save** button
- the **File/Save All** command
- an **Automatic Save** option, which automatically saves documents at regular intervals

In addition to these specific commands, you're automatically asked if you want to save the current version of a document when you attempt to exit Word for Windows, if that document has been modified since the last time it was saved.

This may seem like an awful lot of procedures for what is, to be honest, an obvious activity. The availability of so many alternatives points out how important saving your work can be. A good rule of thumb to apply to any computer project you're involved with, regardless of the application program you're using, is: *Save it once; save it often.*

Quick Saves

The **File/Save** command (**Shift+F12**) and Toolbar **Save** button let you quickly save the current document, using its default name, directory location, and file format. We've used these procedures before, so this is all I'll say about them now.

Save As Options

We've used the **File/Save As** command (**F12**), also. However, it contains some additional options we've not yet discussed. Let's do this now:

1. Select **File** from the Word for Windows Menu bar.
2. Select **Save As**.

This displays the **Save As** dialog box shown in Figure 10.1. One obvious use for this dialog box is to save a second copy of the current document, using a new name. You can also use the **Directories** and **Drives**

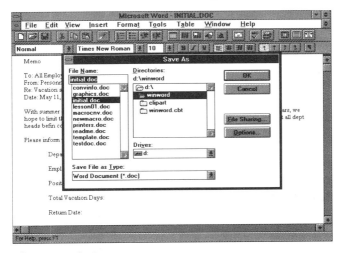

Figure 10.1   The Save As dialog box

list boxes to save the file in a new location, a procedure discussed in Lesson 7.

Next, let me show you a Word for Windows feature you may not know about.

> Point to the down arrow to the right of the **Save File as Type** drop-down list box.

This displays the list box in Figure 10.2. This **Save As** option allows you to take one of your Word for Windows documents and save it in a different file format so that someone who uses, for example, the Macintosh version of Word can work on the same document on his or her computer. This option also can be used to "strip" the various formatting codes from a Word for

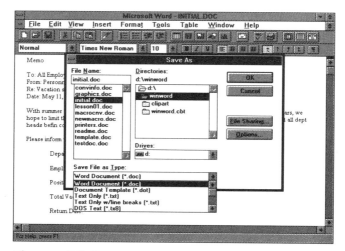

Figure 10.2 You can save your Word for Windows documents in a variety of file formats.

Windows document and convert it into standard (ASCII) text.

The **Save As** dialog box contains other useful options, as well.

Click on the **Options** button.

Selecting Options displays the dialog box in Figure 10.3. It is used to specify save procedures for the current document. The **Save As** options include:

Always Create   Activating this option causes
Backup Copy   Word for Windows to create a
                           copy of the previously saved ver-
                           sion of a document (identified
                           by the file extension **BAK**) each
                           time you save a new version.

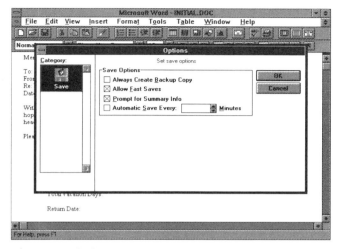

Figure 10.3 The Save As Options dialog box

Allow Fast Saves

Word for Windows saves files in one of two ways: a normal (complete) save and a fast save. A normal save is performed the first time you save a document, and only intermittently after that. The rest of the time, Word for Windows speeds up save operations by performing a fast save, which only records the modifications that have been made to a file since the previous save. Turning off this option forces Word for Windows to perform a normal save each time you save a document. Word for Windows always performs a normal save, regardless of the setting in this field, if the Always Create Backup Copy option is activated.

Prompt for Summary Info	When this option is active, Word for Windows displays its **Summary Info** dialog box the first time you save a document.
Automatic Save Every	Use this option to direct Word for Windows to automatically save changes to your document at specified time intervals. Activating automatic saves is the best way to guarantee that you'll never lose work.

Let's activate the last option—Automatic Save Every—and then exit the **Save As** dialog box.

1. Click on the check box to the left of the **Automatic Save Every** option.
2. Click the up or down arrow to the right of the **Automatic Save Every** option until an appropriate number of minutes is displayed. (The default is 10.)
3. Click on **OK**.
4. When the **Save As** dialog box reappears, click on **OK**.

Tip

These settings also can be set using the **Options** command, located on the pull-down **Tools** menu. This second method lets you modify the file-save options without being forced to perform a **Save As** operation.

Recording Summary Information

Before moving on, let's save our draft memo under a new name.

1. Select **File** from the Menu bar.
2. Select **Save As**.
3. When the the **Save As** dialog box appears, enter **my_memo.doc** in the File Name field.
4. Click on **OK**.

Before saving the new file to disk, Word for Windows displays the **Summary Info** dialog box shown in Figure 10.4. The ability to record summary information about your Word for Windows documents overcomes one of DOS's greatest weaknesses: the fact that it

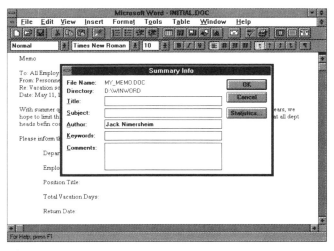

Figure 10.4 The Summary Info dialog box is used to describe a file.

limits file names to 11 characters. Instead of having to remember what a file called **my_memo.doc** contains, you can describe its contents. Additionally, the Keywords field can be used to enter one or more descriptive words to help you find this document quickly using a **Find File** command. As an exercise, insert the following:

1. Type **Vacation memo** and press **Tab**.
2. Type **Coordinating vacation schedules** and press **Tab** twice. (This skips the Author field, into which Word for Windows has already inserted the name you entered during installation.)
3. Type **vacations personnel employees** and press **Tab**.
4. Type **Includes form for recording vacation schedules**.

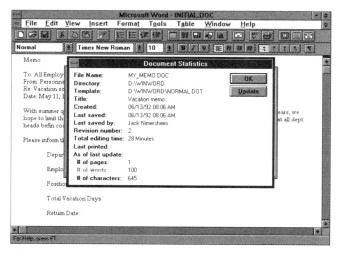

Figure 10.5   The Document Statistics window

We could save this document now, using the summary information just entered. Before doing so, however, let's check out one more Word for Windows feature.

Click on the **Statistics** command button.

Choosing Statistics displays the message window shown in Figure 10.5. Information in this window helps you track the progress of your work.

Now let's save the sample memo, using its new name.

1. Click on **OK** to return to the **Summary Info** dialog box.
2. Click on **OK**.

This saves the memo in a file called **my_memo**. To repeat, saving your work is one of the most critical activities you can perform. The alternative is losing it—not a very attractive option, to be sure.

◆ *Lesson* ◆

11

Opening and Closing Documents

After starting Word for Windows, you can move documents in and out of memory, as needed. This is similar to moving materials pertaining to different projects around on your desk—something you're likely to do quite often throughout the course of a typical day. Furthermore, if you're like most people, you probably work on more than one project at the same time. Recognizing how important the ability to do this is, Word for Windows lets you load several files into memory concurrently. In this lesson we'll examine the commands used to open and close Word for Windows documents.

Closing a Document

Let's begin our imaginary workday with a clean slate, so to speak.

1. Select **File** from the Word for Windows Menu bar.
2. Select the **Close** option.

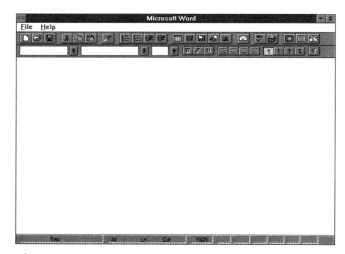

Figure 11.1   Closing all documents in Word for Windows is like clearing your desk.

Three things should have happened, as illustrated in Figure 11.1. First, the Word for Windows workspace no longer contains the **my_memo.doc** file. Second, all but two options, **File** and **Help**, were removed from the Menu bar. Finally, most of the fields in the status line are now blank, because your workspace is empty. Therefore, Word for Windows no longer has any information to display about your relative location within a document.

▷ **Note:** Because we haven't made any changes to **my_memo.doc** since saving it in the previous lesson, your workspace was cleared immediately. If we had modified the document, Word for Windows would have displayed a prompt box before executing the **Close** command, asking if you wanted to save your changes.

Opening a New Document

Of course, an empty desk is a nonproductive desk. So, let's start filling our Word for Windows "desk" up again.

1. Select **File** from the Word for Windows Menu bar.
2. Select the **New** option.

Selecting **New** displays the dialog box shown in Figure 11.2. From this dialog box you select a template to use to create the new document. A template is a blueprint,

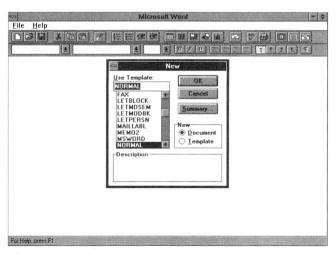

Figure 11.2 The New dialog box

of sorts, which defines the basic design of a document. The information stored in a template includes margin settings, column layout, page orientation, headings (if any), frequently used paragraph formats, and the like.

In some cases, templates provide instructions and assistance to a user, as he or she creates a specific type of document. In this way, templates can be used to standardize similar documents, a process called *boilerplating*. When first starting out, you'll probably use Word for Windows NORMAL template—a very generic yet flexible document format—for the majority of your documents. Over time, however, you'll almost certainly find yourself using some of the other templates initially listed in the **New** dialog box. In all likelihood, in fact, you'll ultimately end up creating new templates designed around your needs.

To familiarize yourself with some of the templates that ship with Word for Windows:

1. Use the arrow keys to highlight different templates in the **Use Template** window.
2. As you highlight a new template, notice the information in the **Description** window of the **New** dialog box.

To see how a template looks:

1. Highlight **MEMO2** in the **Use Template** window.
2. Click on **OK**.

Word for Windows loads the template and begins an automated routine designed to help you write a standard business memo. As part of this routine, the program even lets you specify the people to whom the finished memo should be distributed, as shown in Fig-

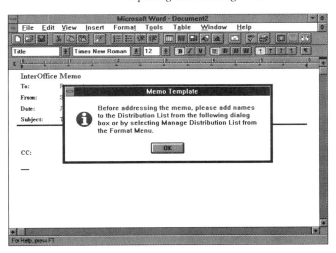

Figure 11.3 Templates can be used to automate frequently used procedures.

ure 11.3. This is an example of what I mentioned earlier, where a template is designed to actually help you complete a specific task.

Our goal here, however, is to learn how to open documents. Templates are another topic that exceed the scope of this book. Still, this gives you an idea of what templates are and how they work. For now:

1. Click on **OK**.
2. When the **Distribution List Manager** dialog box appears, click on **Close**.
3. At the next message box, click on **OK**.
4. At the **From:** dialog box, click on **Cancel**.
5. When Word for Windows asks if you want to stop addressing the memo, click on **Yes**.
6. At the next instruction window, click on **OK**.

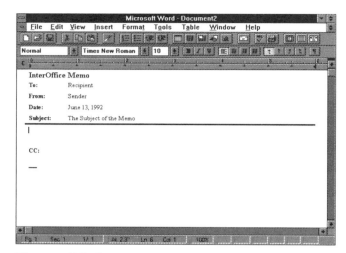

Figure 11.4 A template can serve as a "blueprint" for a new document.

When you've finished, your screen should resemble Figure 11.4, which shows the **MEMO2** template loaded and ready to use. We will use it later. For now, however, leave it loaded into the Word for Windows workspace and return to the sample memo, which we've been working on throughout the previous lessons.

Opening an Existing Document

Word for Windows lets you work with more than one document at the same time. To see what I mean:

1. Select **File** from the Word for Windows Menu bar.
2. Select the **Open** option.

Word for Windows displays its **Open** dialog box. You've seen this dialog box already, in Lesson 5. At that time, we opened our sample memo quickly, without really discussing how the **Open** function worked. Let's eliminate this oversight now.

The most common use of the **Open** dialog box is to reload document files created with Word for Windows, as we did in Lesson 5. It can do much more, however. During installation, Setup transferred a number of file-conversion utilities from the Word for Windows distribution diskettes to your hard disk. These conversion utilities allow you to take files created with other applications and convert them into Word for Windows documents. In many ways, this process is the reverse of the **Save File As Type** feature discussed in the previous lesson, which allowed you to translate a Word for Windows document into a file format that would be recognized by another application.

Whenever you attempt to open a file that was created with another program, Word for Windows displays the **Convert File** dialog box shown in Figure 11.5. Selecting the appropriate file format from this list will run the corresponding utility and convert the original file into a Word for Windows document. The availability of these conversion utilities means you don't have to discard all the work you may have done previously with other application programs as you switch over to using Word for Windows.

For now, we'll simply load our sample document, which does not require conversion.

1. Click on **my_memo.doc** in the File Name listing.
2. Click on **OK**.

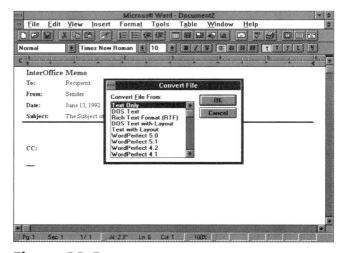

Figure 11.5 It's easy to convert files created with other programs into Word for Windows documents.

In a few seconds you'll see our familiar memo. Keep in mind, however, that we have other documents loaded into memory, as well. And we'll get back to them shortly. Before then, however, we're going to look at the commands used to print a Word for Windows document.

12
Previewing Your Document

In just a few moments, we're going to print our sample memo. Before actually printing a document, however, it's always a good idea to review its general appearance. Word for Windows provides an easy way to do this.

1. Select **File** from the Word for Windows Menu bar.
2. Select the **Print Preview** option.

Print Preview displays a representation of your printed document on the screen, as shown in Figure 12.1. This allows you to analyze its general layout—margins, balance, placement of text, and so forth. Should you see any glaring faults, you can then go back to the regular Word for Windows display and correct them.

For longer documents, Print Preview provides a way to preview two pages so you can determine how they will look side by side.

Click on the **Two Pages** command button.

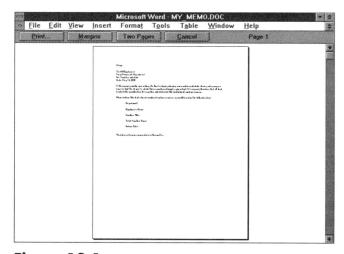

Figure 12.1 Use Print Preview to preview the appearance of a printed document.

Your screen should now resemble Figure 12.2, which shows a two-page Print Preview display. Of course, given the brevity of our sample memo, the second page in this screen is blank.

For the most part, Page Preview is a static display; that is, it does not allow you to make major modification to your document. One thing you can do from within Page Preview, however, is adjust margin settings and page breaks. To see how this is done:

1. Click on the **One Page** command button.
2. Click on the **Margins** command button.

Your display should now resemble Figure 12.3. This figure contains a series of lines representing the margin settings for the current document. Additionally, a hor-

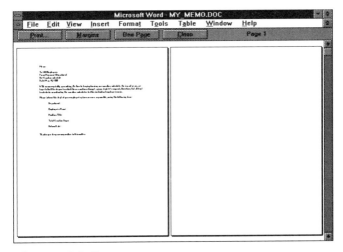

Figure 12.2 A two-page view let's you preview longer documents.

izontal line just below the last line of the memo represents a page break, in this case the end of our short document.

Now try the following experiment:

1. Position the mouse pointer over the box located at the bottom of the right-hand margin line. This causes the arrow to turn into a plus sign, resembling a cross hair.
2. Hold down the left mouse button. Notice that the page number, previously displayed to the right of the command buttons, is replaced with **1.25"**. This indicates the current setting of the right margin—printing stops 1.25" from the right-hand side of the page.

3. Drag the mouse slightly to the left, until this setting changes to **1.5"**.

4. Release the left mouse button. This causes Word for Windows to redisplay the right margin line at the new setting, **1.5"** from the right-hand side of the page. Notice that some of the text in the second line of the main paragraph extends beyond the new margin setting.

5. Press **Enter**. This tells Word for Windows to accept the new margin. Look carefully, and you'll notice that the paragraph has been reformatted to match the current setting. You can use this same "drag" technique, followed by **Enter**, to adjust any of the margins or page breaks during a Print Preview.

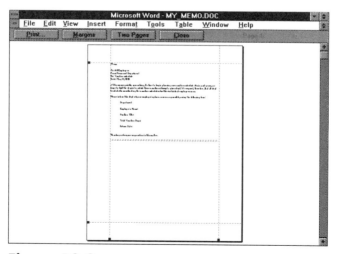

Figure 12.3 You can adjust margins and page breaks in Page Preview.

As you've probably guessed, selecting the **Print** button causes Word for Windows to print the memo immediately. Instead, however, let's leave Page Preview. That way, we'll be able to examine all the printing features of Word for Windows in the next lesson.

Click on the **Close** command button.

This closes Print Preview and returns you to the main Word for Windows workspace.

13

Printing a Document

Okay, it's time to take that sample memo and transform it from pixels on a computer terminal into printed words on a piece of paper. This, after all, is what word processing is all about.

The Print Option

Printing with any Windows application, including Word for Windows, is a breeze. To begin printing our sample memo:

1. Select **File** from the Word for Windows Menu bar.
2. Select the **Print** option.

This displays the **Print** dialog box, shown in Figure 13.1, used to specify information about the current print operation.

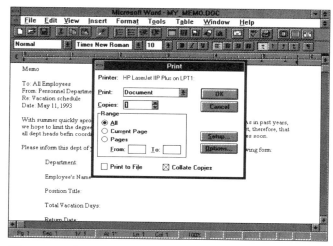

Figure 13.1   The Print dialog box

The following items are specified in the **Print** dialog box:

- which printer Windows should use (the default is the current system printer)
- a drop-down list box from which you can select what you want to print (the default is the current document)
- how many copies of the current document you want to print (the default is 1)
- a **Range** option that you use to indicate how much of a document you want to print (the default is All)
- a check box that can be used to print the document to a disk file, rather than the printer

- a check box that can be used to indicate whether you want pages collated (that is, placed in their proper order) as they're printed (the default is Collate Copies)

Clicking on the **OK** button now would print the current document using all the default values. Using common Windows techniques, you can change any default settings in the **Print** dialog box, if desired.

Setting Additional Print Options

A second set of options gives you even more control over the appearance and contents of your Word for Windows documents during printing. To access these settings:

Click on the **Options** command button.

This displays a dialog box containing additional Word for Windows print options, as shown in Figure 13.2. Some of these settings affect all Word for Windows print operations. Others, specifically those in the bottom box, apply only to the current document.

Tip

This second set of print options is available at any time during a Word for Windows session. To access them, select **Options** from the **Tools** menu.

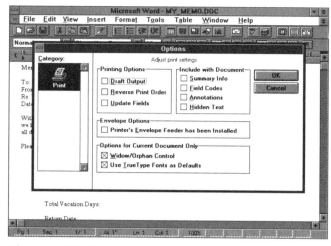

Figure 13.2 Additional print options

A few of the options in this second dialog box deserve mention:

Draft Output   Choosing this option prints only the text of your document, without full formatting. Because printing drafts takes much less time than printing final copies, you should use this option to print a document for review and copy editing.

Reverse Print Order   Some printers eject pages in reverse order, causing you to end up with your pages stacked from last to first. Selecting this option circumvents this problem.

Widow/Orphan Widows and orphans are short
Control lines or single words that appear
as the last or first line at the bottom or top of a printed page, respectively. Because widows and
orphans are considered unac-
ceptable in most documents, the
default setting eliminates them.

For our purposes, we'll leave the default settings
unchanged. So, let's print our memo.

1. Click on **Cancel** to remove the **Options** dialog
   box.
2. Click on the **OK** command button.

Word for Windows displays the message box shown in
Figure 13.3, indicating that printing has begun. Now

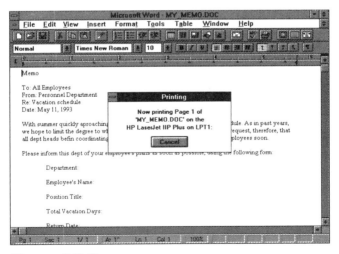

Figure 13.3   Printing in progress

you're probably wondering, "Why isn't my printer running?" The answer to this question leads to a discussion of one of Windows most useful features, its Print Manager.

Print Manager

As mentioned earlier, Windows itself assumes responsibility for coordinating printing. It does this using Print Manager, a special Windows utility that organizes and controls the print operations for all your Windows applications. Figure 13.4 shows Print Manager in action.

Notice that our sample memo, **my_memo.doc**, has been added to a list of documents that are being printed. This is called a print queue. Because Print Manager runs in the background of other Windows applications, you regain control of Word for Windows much more quickly than would be possible if it had to coordinate the printing of your documents. In fact, it should only have taken a few seconds to send **my_memo.doc** to Print Manager, after which you were returned to the main Word for Windows display.

Print Manager lets you adjust its operations and modify the print queue, should you ever want to do so.

Figure 13.4   Word for Windows transfers the requested print operation to Print Manager.

The *Word for Windows User's Guide* contains information about how to use Print Manager.

Once you're back at the main Word for Windows display, you could continue working, even as your document prints. For now, however, why don't you take a break and wait for Print Manager to print your initial memo? I'm sure you're eager to see it. When you're finished perusing your handiwork, move on to the next lesson. After all, we still have a lot of ground to cover before we're done.

14

Working With Multiple Documents

Just a few more mechanics and then we're ready to begin really sprucing up the sample memo. You may recall that, in Lesson 11, we left a business memo template open in our Word for Windows environment. I told you then we'd get back to it shortly. Well, "shortly" has arrived.

Viewing Multiple Documents

Managing more than one document is not unlike working with a single, long document, something we did in Lesson 5. The biggest difference is that, rather than using multiple windows to access different portions of the same file, you're actually making changes to two or more files concurrently. To see what I mean:

1. Select **Window** from the Word for Windows Menu bar.
2. Select the **Arrange All** option.

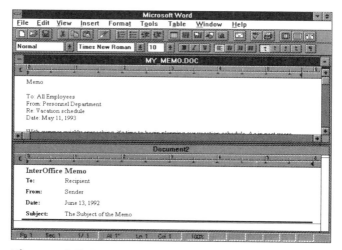

Figure 14.1 Word for Windows lets you display multiple documents concurrently.

Your screen should now resemble Figure 14.1, which shows **my_memo.doc** and the business memo template, currently called **Document2**, equally sharing the Word for Windows display. Word for Windows lets you open up to nine display windows—containing either parts of a document, multiple documents, or some combination of the two—at any given time.

Resizing Document Windows

An equally divided screen is not always the best way to work with multiple files, however. There may be times when you want to modify your document windows to a more convenient arrangement. The easiest way to accomplish this is by using the mouse to adjust the size and location of one or more windows. Try this:

1. Click on the title bar of **Document2** to make this the active window.
2. Move the mouse pointer near the line dividing the two display windows until it changes into a double-headed arrow.
3. Hold down the left mouse button.
4. Drag your mouse upward until the resulting shaded line is located just below the line in **my_memo.doc** that reads "From: Personnel Department."
5. Release the left mouse button.

This enlarges the Document2 window by moving its top border to the selected location, as illustrated in Figure 14.2. Now:

1. Move the mouse pointer to the far right border of the Document2 window.
2. Hold down the left mouse button.
3. Drag your mouse to the left and upward until the resulting shaded line is lined up with the 4 in the Document2 ruler bar.
4. Release the left mouse button.

Your display should now resemble Figure 14.3, which shows the Document2 window reduced.

Now we're going to get tricky, so pay attention.

1. Move the mouse pointer to the bottom border of the **my_memo.doc** window.
2. Hold down the left mouse button.

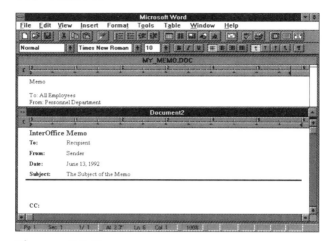

Figure 14.2 Dragging a top or bottom border modifies the height of a window.

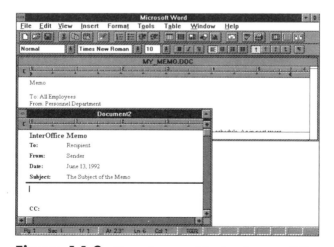

Figure 14.3 Dragging a side border modifies the width of a window.

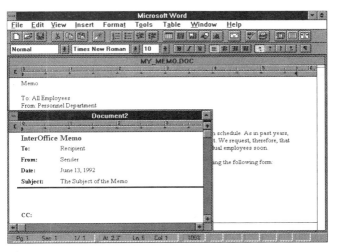

Figure 14.4 With some fine-tuning, you can set up almost any display arrangement you want.

3. Drag your mouse downward until the resulting shaded line is lined up with the 4 in the Document2 Ruler bar.
4. Release the left mouse button.
5. Select **Window** from the Word for Windows Menu bar.
6. Select **Document2** from the **Window** pull-down menu.

Figure 14.4 shows the results of this exercise.

Moving a Window

Another way to rearrange your Word for Windows display is by moving windows around. This is not unlike picking up a file folder and setting it down in a new location. To see what I mean:

1. Position the mouse pointer over the title of the **Document2** window.
2. Hold down the left mouse button.
3. Drag your mouse to the left and up until the resulting outline box is located in the upper right-hand corner of the **my_memo.doc** window.
4. Release the left mouse button.

Figure 14.5 shows the result of this move.

As these few examples demonstrate, there's almost no limit on the degree to which you can personalize your Word for Windows display. That's one of the

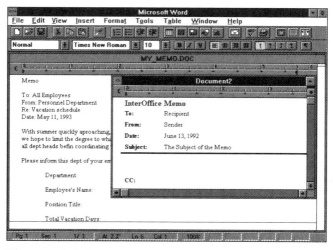

Figure 14.5   You can move individual windows.

primary attractions of working in a graphics-based environment like Windows.

But Word for Windows is about more than mechanics. It's also about making your documents so professional looking that people will think they were designed by a professional typesetter. Those are the Word for Windows features we'll be examining in *Part II* of this book, "Refining Your Skills." And the fun begins in the next lesson. Before moving on, however, let's clean up our current workspace.

1. Click on the Control box to the left of the **Document2** Title bar.
2. Choose **Close** from the pull-down Control menu.
3. Select **No** when Word asks if you want to save the changes to this document.

This closes the **Document2** window and leaves **my_memo.doc** the only open document.

PART II

REFINING YOUR
SKILLS

◆ *Lesson* ◆

15

Manipulating Blocks of Text

To paraphrase Thomas A. Edison: "Successful writing requires 1 percent inspiration and 99 percent perspiration." The inspiration part generally produces the first draft of a document. The remaining 99 percent of the writing process involves polishing this draft to perfection, or what writers often refer to as the dreaded edit phase.

Any good word processing program eliminates some of the sweat from the 99 percent part of writing. Word for Windows makes it especially easy. In this lesson we begin examining those Word for Windows features that allow you to modify the content and appearance of your documents. We'll start by describing the procedures used to select and manipulate blocks of text.

Selecting Blocks of Text

Word for Windows provides several ways to select, or mark, a block of text for additional processing. Which method you use depends on how much text you want to mark.

- To select a single word, double-click on that word.
- To select multiple words, hold down the left mouse button as you drag your mouse over the words you want to select.
- To select an entire sentence, point to anywhere within the sentence, hold down the **Ctrl** key and click the left mouse button.
- To select a display line, click on the selection bar (the far-left portion of your display) next to the desired line.
- To select a paragraph, double-click on the selection bar next to any line within the desired paragraph.
- To select multiple paragraphs, hold down the left mouse button as you drag your mouse over the paragraphs you want to select.
- To select an entire document, point to the selection bar then hold down the **Ctrl** key and click the left mouse button.
- To select any irregular block of text, point to the beginning of the block you want to select and click the left mouse button. Then, point to the end of the block you want to select and, while holding down the **Shift** key, click the left mouse button.

Using "Drag-and-Drop" to Move Marked Text

Once a block of text is marked, you can manipulate it in a variety of ways. Many of these relate to document formatting—setting margins, selecting text characteristics, and so forth—which we'll take up in subsequent lessons. Right now, we'll concentrate on marking text for so-called "cut-and-paste" procedures.

1. Click on the selection bar to the left of the **Date:** line at the beginning of our sample memo.
2. Point to the "D" at the beginning of the word "Date".
3. Hold down the left mouse button.
4. Drag the mouse pointer up three lines, until the resulting vertical line is located just before the "T" in "To:".
5. Release the left mouse button.

Your screen should now resemble Figure 15.1, in which the Date line has been moved to the beginning

Figure 15.1 "Drag-and-drop" lets you quickly move selected text to a new location.

of our sample memo. This illustrates a common mouse technique called "drag-and-drop." In essence, after selecting the Date line, you dragged it to a new position. Releasing the mouse button "dropped" the selected line back into our memo at this new location.

Using the Windows Clipboard

Drag-and-drop works fine when moving text blocks short distances. For more complicated operations, you may want to rely on the Windows Clipboard. Stated simply, you use the Clipboard to temporarily store data for additional processing.

Figure 15.2   The Edit menu

With the "Date:" line still highlighted, click on **Edit** in the Word for Windows Menu bar to display the pull-down Edit menu shown in Figure 15.2. The second section of the menu contains several options used to move marked text to and from the Windows Clipboard. These include:

- Cut—deletes marked text from the active window and transfers it to the Clipboard.
- Copy—leaves the marked text in the active window, but creates a copy of it in the Clipboard.
- Paste—inserts the current contents of the Clipboard into the active window.
- Paste Special—creates a dynamic link between data in the Clipboard and the active window; in this way, changes made in one window are reflected in other windows.

To see how the Clipboard works:

1. Select **Cut** from the Edit menu. This removes the "Date:" line from the memo and places it in the Windows Clipboard.
2. Point to the beginning of the blank line directly below the "Re:" line of the sample memo.
3. Click on **Edit** in the Word for Windows Menu bar. (Because the Clipboard now contains data, the Paste option is active.)
4. Select the **Paste** option.

Voila! Windows reinserts the "Date:" line at the specified location.

Tip

The following keyboard shortcuts are available for cut-and-paste operations:

- **Ctrl-X** or **Del**—moves marked text to the Clipboard (Cut).
- **Ctrl-C**—copies marked text to the Clipboard (Copy).
- **Ctrl-V**—transfers the current contents of the Clipboard to the active window (Paste).

USING CLIPBOARD TO TRANSFER DATA BETWEEN DOCUMENTS

The Clipboard also provides a convenient method for transferring data between windows. These can include other Windows applications or, alternately, multiple windows running under the same application. To see how this works, try the following:

1. Select **File** from the Word for Windows Menu bar.
2. Select the **New** option.
3. At the **New** dialog box, click on **OK**.
4. Select **Window** from the Word for Windows Menu bar.
5. Select the **MY_MEMO.DOC** option.
6. Use the selection bar to mark the five lines used to record vacation information: Department, Employee's Name, Position Title, Total Vacation Days, and Return Date.
7. Select **Edit** from the Menu bar.

Figure 15.3 The Clipboard lets you create dynamic links between documents.

8. Select the **Copy** option.
9. Select **Window** from the Menu bar.
10. Select the **Document2** option.
11. Select **Edit** from the Menu bar.
12. Select the **Paste Special** option.
13. At the Paste Special dialog box, select **Paste Link**.

Step 12 displayed the Paste Special dialog box shown in Figure 15.3. In Step 13, you used this dialog box to establish a dynamic link between the marked section of **my_memo.doc** and a second Word for Windows document. (You may not have realized it, but you created a second document in Steps 2 and 3, above.)

Before moving on, let's save our new document for future use.

1. Select **File** from the Word for Windows Menu bar.
2. Select **Save** from the File menu.
3. Name this new file **vac_form.doc**.
4. Enter the following information into the Summary Info dialog box:

   Title: **Vacation Schedule Form**
   Subject: **1992 vacation schedules**
   Comments: **Form for recording information about employee's vacation schedule.**

5. Click on **OK**.

In this lesson, we examined the procedures used to mark and manipulate text blocks. At the same time, we laid the groundwork for discussions and exercises in subsequent lessons.

16

Searching for and Replacing Text

You've already seen the Find command in action. We used it in Lesson 7 to demonstrate how dialog boxes work. In this lesson, we'll examine additional ways that you can find and, if desired, automatically replace text within a Word for Windows document.

Using the Go To Command

To prepare for the following exercises, we must first return to the beginning of **my_memo.doc**. Therefore:

1. Select **Window** from the Word for Windows Menu bar.
2. Choose **my_memo.doc**.
3. Select **Edit** from the Word for Windows Menu bar.
4. Select the **Go To** option.

Selecting Go To displays the Go To dialog box shown in Figure 16.1. The Go To command is especially useful when you're working in long files. It lets you quickly move to a different location within the active docu-

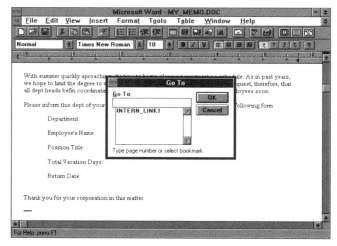

Figure 16.1   The Go To dialog box

ment, including a specific page. We'll use Go To to position the insertion point at the beginning of page one.

1. Type **1**.
2. Click on **OK**.

Using the ? Wildcard

Now that we're where we want to be, let's look at a feature Word for Windows borrows from DOS: the wildcard character. The ability to include wildcards in a Find command lets you search for a word or phrase, even if you don't know its exact contents.

1. Select **Edit** from the Word for Windows Menu bar.
2. Select the **Find** option.

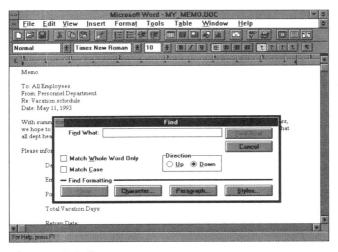

Figure 16.2 The Find dialog box

This displays the Find dialog box shown in Figure 16.2. In Lesson 7, we used this dialog box to find a specific word. But what if you're not certain of how the word you're looking for is spelled? Suppose, for example, that you recognize from past experience that you often use the words "cooperation" and "corporation" interchangeably in your writing. How could you quickly scan a document to make sure it doesn't contain this error? That's where the question mark (**?**) wildcard comes in handy. Try the following:

1. Type **co???ration** in the Find What box.
2. Click on **OK**.

Sure enough, as illustrated in Figure 16.3, Word for Windows finds and highlights "corporation," which was used incorrectly within our sample memo. We

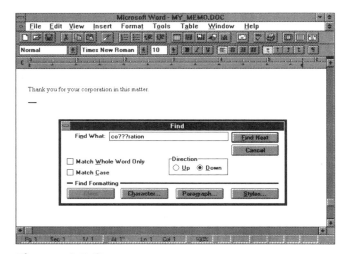

Figure 16.3 Wildcards let you find text using a partial search string.

could fix this now, but why not let Word for Windows do it for us?

Find and Replace

Like most word processors, Word for Windows lets you automatically replace one word or phrase with another word or phrase. Let's use this feature to clear up our corporation/cooperation confusion.

1. Click on **Cancel** to remove the Find dialog box.
2. Use **Edit/Go To** to return to the top of page 1.
3. Select **Edit** from the Word for Windows Menu bar.
4. Select the **Replace** option.

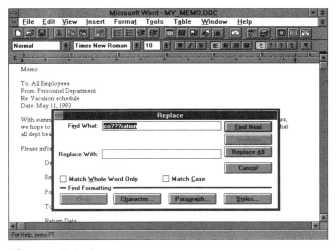

Figure 16.4 The Replace dialog box

Word for Windows displays its Replace dialog box. (See Figure 16.4.) The Find and Replace dialog boxes are similar to one another, except that the latter has an additional field, **Replace With**. You use this extra field to enter a new word or phrase you want to substitute for the text string in the Find What field during a find-and-replace operation. Try this now:

1. Press **Tab** to advance the insert point to the Replace With field.
2. Type **cooperation**.
3. Click on **Find Next**.
4. When Word for Windows finds the incorrect word, click on **Replace**.

Did it work? Let's find out.

1. Click on **Cancel** to remove the Replace dialog box.
2. Click on the vertical scroll bar to display the bottom of **my_memo.doc**.

Word for Windows corrected the previous error, fixing our sample memo. Well, we've corrected one part of our memo. Of course, you realize there are still more errors to correct. Don't worry. They'll be taken care of in the next lesson.

17

Checking Spelling and Grammar

Word for Windows includes three important writing tools to help ensure that your documents are as close to perfect as they can be:

- a spell checker
- a grammar checker
- a thesaurus

Used wisely, each of these tools can be used to improve both the content and clarity of your writing.

Using the Spell Checker

To begin cleaning up our sample memo, let's see if Word for Windows can help us find any misspellings it contains.

1. Click on the top of the vertical scroll bar to return to the beginning of the document.
2. Select **Tools** from the Word for Windows Menu bar.
3. Select the **Spelling** option.

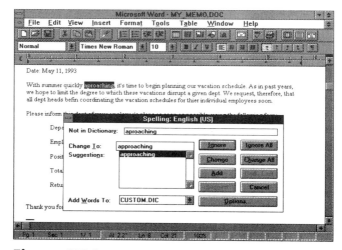

Figure 17.1   Word for Windows helps uncover potential spelling errors in your document.

Selecting the Spelling option causes Word for Windows to begin comparing the contents of the current document with its built-in dictionary. Every time Word for Windows encounters a word it doesn't recognize, it pauses the spell check and displays the dialog box shown in Figure 17.1.

You can take one of three actions when Word for Windows encounters a potential misspelling:

1. Ignore the flagged word.
2. Replace the flagged word with a word shown in the **Suggestions** box.
3. Eliminate a misspelling manually by typing the correct word into the **Change To** text box.

The spelling checker also detects repeated words (the the) and unusual capitalization (JAck). A fourth option, Delete, is added to the Spelling dialog box when the former condition exists.

In this case, the flagged word in Figure 17.1 is definitely misspelled. To correct it:

Select **Change**.

The next potential misspelling Word for Windows detects is "dept," an abbreviation for department that I used several times when writing the sample memo. Using such shortcuts allows you to write first drafts quickly. You can then go back and have Word for Windows "fill in the blanks," so to speak, as you polish your document.

1. Type **department** into the **Change To** field.
2. Select **Change All**.

Tip
You could also use the Replace command, introduced in the previous lesson, to spell out abbreviations and other shorthand notations.

Go ahead and finish the spelling check on your own, but I'll give you a hint: Two more misspellings exist in the initial draft of our sample memo.

After scanning the entire document, Word for Windows displays the dialog box shown in Figure 17.2.

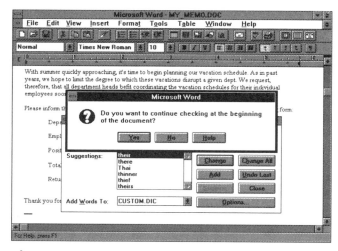

Figure 17.2 Word for Windows lets you know when the entire document has been checked.

Selecting **Yes** at this dialog box would initiate a second pass on the current document. For now:

Choose **No**.

This ends the current spelling check and returns you to the document.

> **Note:** The Word for Windows spell checker works by comparing your document to the contents of its built-in dictionary. Every word that shows up during a spell check, therefore, is not necessarily misspelled. For example, a surname or company name will usually cause Word for Windows to inquire about spelling, unless you add it

to your personal dictionary by clicking the Add Option and then typing in the word.

Checking Grammar

The **Grammar** option in the Tools menu checks for potential grammatical errors within a document. The grammar checker works much like the spell checker. It stops whenever it encounters a questionable passage and gives you an opportunity to correct it. Figure 17.3, for example, shows the dialog box Word for Windows displays when it discovers a subject/verb disagreement in our sample document.

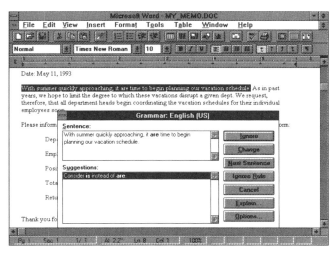

Figure 17.3 Word for Windows helps you detect potential grammatical errors in your documents.

Running a grammar check is a good idea, even if your document is grammatically flawless. To see why:

1. If necessary, position the insertion point at the beginning of the sample memo.
2. Select **Tools** from the Word for Windows menu bar.
3. Select the **Grammar** option.

Following each grammar check, Word for Windows displays the Readability Statistics message box shown in Figure 17.4. This box contains useful information about the section of a document on which a grammar check is performed, in this case, the entire memo.

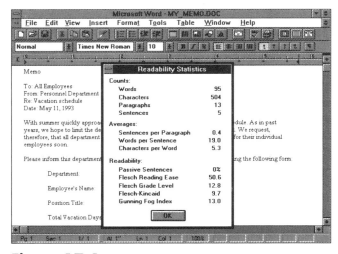

Figure 17.4 A grammar check also analyzes the contents of your documents.

Analyzing the contents of this message box will help guarantee that your writing is appropriate for the target audience. You wouldn't want a children's newsletter, for example, to return the Flesch Grade Level rating of 12.8 (equivalent to college freshman) shown in Figure 17.4.

After reviewing this information:

Click on **OK** to end the grammar check and return to your document.

Using the Thesaurus

Writing well involves much more than mere mechanics. Effective writing also includes your choice of language. Word for Windows built-in thesaurus helps you pick the right word for the right circumstances. For example, the word "begin" appears twice in the main paragraph of our sample memo. While such repetition is not necessarily wrong, substituting a different word in one of these locations may be a better choice. To make the substitution:

1. Double-click on **begin** in the first sentence of this paragraph.
2. Select **Tools** from the Word for Windows Menu bar.
3. Select the **Thesaurus** option. Word for Windows displays the dialog box shown in Figure 17.5, which you use to choose a synonym for the selected word.
4. Click on **start** in the **Synonyms** box.
5. Click on **Replace**.

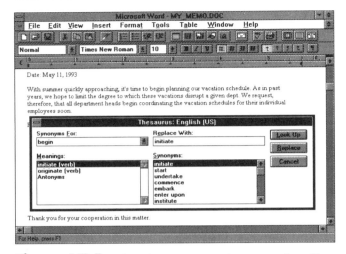

Figure 17.5   The Thesaurus can improve the effectiveness of your writing.

Word for Windows replaces the selected word with the specified synonym.

While these tools and utilities are no substitute for a knowledge of the English language and well-developed writing skills, the Word for Windows spell checker, grammar checker, and thesaurus can help you polish your document.

◆ *Lesson* ◆

18

Setting Document Margins

While it's true that, as the popular adage proclaims, looks aren't everything, they do count for something. The more professional your documents look, the more likely they are to have the desired effect upon the reader. In this regard also, Word for Windows can help. In this and several subsequent lessons, we'll examine the Word for Windows commands and procedures used to transform simple text into an attractive looking document.

Using the On-Screen Ruler

The Word for Windows Ruler bar makes it easy to modify specific elements of your document. The most obvious of these is a document's margin settings.

When you first start Word for Windows, it uses the Ruler bar to display the absolute width of your document, that is, how many inches wide a document is, regardless of its margin settings. To see what I mean:

If necessary, use the **View/Ruler** (**Alt-V, R**) command to display Word for Windows on-screen Ruler.

Notice that the text in our sample memo currently occupies the space between 0" and 5.75" within the on-screen rulers. (You may recall that we specified this width from the Print Preview screen, back in Lesson 12.) You can also have the on-screen Ruler indicate the relative width of your document, that is, its positioning on a printed page.

Click on the opening bracket to the far left of the Ruler bar.

The Ruler bar changes to now indicate that the text of our sample memo covers a horizontal distance from 1.25" to 7", relative to the edges of a printed page, as shown in Figure 18.1. A simple calculation reveals that this second ruler display still indicates an overall document width of 5.75" (7 − 1.25 = 5.75).

Changing a Margin Setting

The Ruler bar is much more than a simple indicator, however. You can also use it to change margin settings quickly.

1. Point to the left bracket, which is now located below the 1.25" mark of the on-screen Ruler.
2. Hold down the left mouse button.
3. Drag your mouse to the right until this bracket is located under the 2" mark.
4. Release the left mouse button.

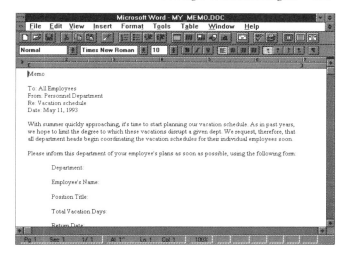

Figure 18.1 The on-screen Ruler can indicate the absolute or relative width of a document.

Your screen should now resemble Figure 18.2. Notice that Word for Windows automatically adjusted your text to fit within the new margin settings.

Formatting Sections of a Document

The previous exercise established new margin settings for the entire sample memo. You can also format a discrete section of your document.

1. Point to the "W" in the word "With" that begins the main paragraph of our sample memo.
2. Click the left mouse button to position the insertion point at the beginning of this paragraph.
3. Select **Insert** from the Menu bar.
4. Select the **Break** option.

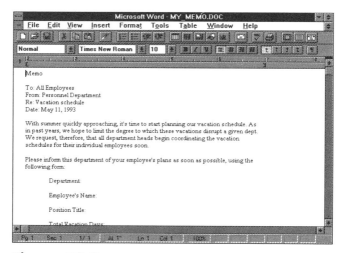

Figure 18.2   Word for Windows automatically adjusts text to the current margin settings.

5. In the **Section Break** portion of the resulting dialog box, click on **Continuous**.
6. Click on **OK**.

Your display should now show a broken line before the main paragraph of our sample memo. This nonprinting line indicates that you selected the Continuous option to insert a section break on the current page. To modify the margin settings for the new section, that is, all text after the beginning of the main paragraph:

1. Place the insertion point anywhere within the new section.
2. Point to the left bracket, which is now located below the 2" mark of the on-screen ruler.
3. Hold down the left mouse button.

4. Drag your mouse to the right until this bracket is located under the 2.5" mark.

5. Release the left mouse button.

You may think nothing happened. After all, your display still shows both the beginning of the memo and the new section lined up with one another. But to see what actually happened:

1. Select **View** from the Word for Windows Menu bar.

2. Select the **Page Layout** option.

Your screen should now resemble Figure 18.3. Changing to the Page Layout view caused Word for Windows

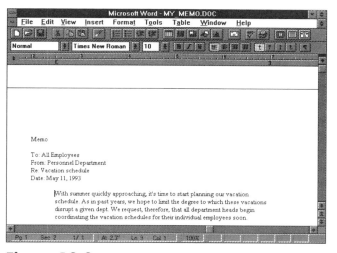

Figure 18.3 The Page Layout view shows the results of our reformatting.

to adjust its display to reflect the printed appearance of the sample memo, including margin settings.

Be aware that selecting the Page Layout view slows down Word for Windows somewhat, as opposed to the Normal setting. For now, however, let's keep this view active. Doing so will allow us to monitor more closely the results of our formatting activities over the next few lessons.

19

Setting Tabs

Tabs provide another convenient way to format text. Tab stops let you fill a predetermined space with either printing or nonprinting characters. You can also use tab stops to keep items lined up with one another against an "invisible margin" of sorts.

Inserting Tab Characters

Let's begin by using tabs to insert printing characters in our sample memo.

1. Position the insertion point immediately after the colon that ends the indented line containing **Department:**
2. Select **Format** from the Word for Windows Menu bar.
3. Select the **Tabs** option.

This displays the Tabs dialog box shown in Figure 19.1, which is used to set and format tab stops.

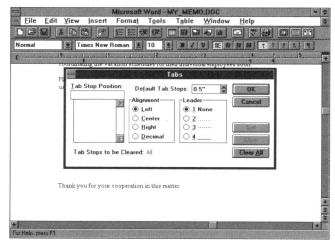

Figure 19.1 Modifying the default tab settings.

Now try the following:

1. Type **4"** in the **Tab Stop Position** text box.
2. Click on **4** (solid line) in the **Leader** options box.
3. Click on **Set**.
4. Click on **OK**.
5. When you return to your document, press **Tab**.

Word for Windows places a solid line following the colon that extends out to the 4" ruler mark.

But the Ruler bar provides an even easier way to adjust tab stops:

1. Position the insertion point immediately after the colon that ends the indented line containing **Employee's Name:**
2. Point to the tab stop marker directly below the 1.5" mark on the Ruler bar.

3. Hold down the left mouse button.
4. Drag your mouse to the right until the pointer is under the 4" ruler mark.
5. Release the left mouse button.
6. Select **Format** from the Word for Windows Menu bar.
7. Select the **Tabs** option.
8. Click on **4** (solid line) in the **Leader** options box.
9. Click on **Set**.
10. Click on **OK**.
11. When you return to your document, press **Tab**.

Different steps, same result. Go ahead and use one of the previous methods to add underlines to the remaining three-form line until your display resembles Figure 19.2.

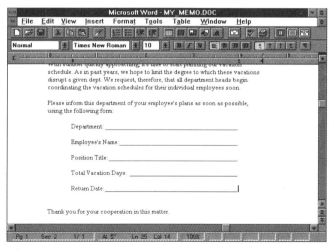

Figure 19.2 The creative use of leading tab characters can create an attractive form.

The tab stops we set in the previous exercises served double duty:

1. By selecting a leading character of a solid line, we added some visual panache to our sample memo.

2. By using a 4" tab stop to mark the end of the leading character, we were able to line up the end of all our underlines precisely four inches in from the left margin in this section of our sample memo.

And we're not finished spiffing up our sample memo yet. Not by a long shot. In the next lesson, we'll make some more subtle changes designed to add to its attractive appearance.

20
Aligning Text

This lesson is going to be short, sweet, and to the point. Alignment refers to how the text in a document lines up with itself and, by extension, the print margins of a page. There are four basic types of alignment:

- left-aligned—individual lines of text line up on the left margin; the right margin is usually uneven (ragged).
- centered—individual lines of text are centered between the left and right margins; both margins are usually uneven.
- right-aligned—individual lines of text line up on the right margin; the left margin is usually uneven.
- justified—individual lines of text line up on both the left and right margins; both margins are even.

The alignment you choose generally depends on what type of document you're creating. Informal documents (personal letters and the like) are usually left-aligned. More formal documents (books, reports, and so forth) are often justified. Right-aligned and centered text is used primarily for design purposes in brochures, advertising material, and the like. Of course, these are informal rules, at best. The secret is to select the alignment that best suits the purpose of your document.

Aligning a Paragraph

For the sake of this exercise, let's assume that we're composing an "official" corporate memo. To have it look as professional as possible, we'll justify the two paragraphs contained in the main body.

1. Use the vertical scroll bar to display the two paragraphs immediately following the introduction on your screen.
2. Double click on the selection bar immediately to the left of the first paragraph.
3. Hold down the **Shift** key and double click on the selection bar immediately to the left of the second paragraph.
4. Select **Format** from the Word for Windows Menu bar.
5. Select the **Paragraph** option.

This displays the Paragraph dialog box shown in Figure 20.1. Use this dialog box to modify formatting for selected paragraphs.

Notice that **Alignment** is currently set to **Left**, the default alignment. Let's change this.

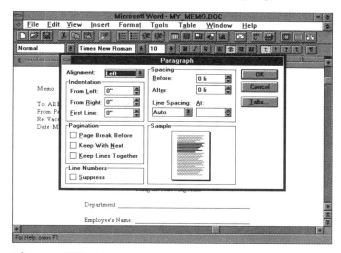

Figure 20.1 The Paragraph dialog box

1. Click on the down arrow to the right of **Alignment** field to display the drop-down box list.
2. Click on **Justified**. (Notice that the representative page in the **Sample** window changes to reflect your new choice.)
3. Click on **OK**.

Your screen should now resemble Figure 20.2. In this figure the selected paragraphs have been reformatted to full justification. (If you're wondering how Word for Windows accomplishes this, here's a hint: Check out the spaces between letters and words in the justified text; these are increased, as needed, to push each line out to the right margin.

Figure 20.2 Word for Windows automatically reformats the selected paragraphs to the specified alignment.

Tip

Believe it or not, there's an even easier way to change alignment. Notice the four alignment buttons located in the Word for Windows Ribbon bar, between the 3" and 4" marks on the Ruler bar. After selecting the paragraphs to be reformatted, clicking the appropriate button in the Ribbon bar—in this case, the alignment button just above the 4" mark—would have accomplished the same thing.

Like I said: short, sweet, and to the point. Now, let's move on.

21

Indenting Text

This lesson explores in more detail a Word for Windows feature you've already encountered. You may recall that we used the Toolbar's Indent button in Lesson 8 to shift the lines requesting specific vacation information one tab stop to the right, so you already know that the Toolbar Indent and Unindent buttons realign entire paragraphs. But it's also possible to indent (or unindent) single lines. Finally, you can define indentations that use increments other than the preset tab marks.

Indenting Single Lines

The Tab key can be used to indent any line within a Word for Windows document. As you may suspect, this method indents the selected text to the preset tab marks on the ruler line. But what if you want to indent a line to a distance other than one of the preset tab marks? Let's see how this is done.

1. Place the insertion point at the beginning of the first paragraph in our sample memo.

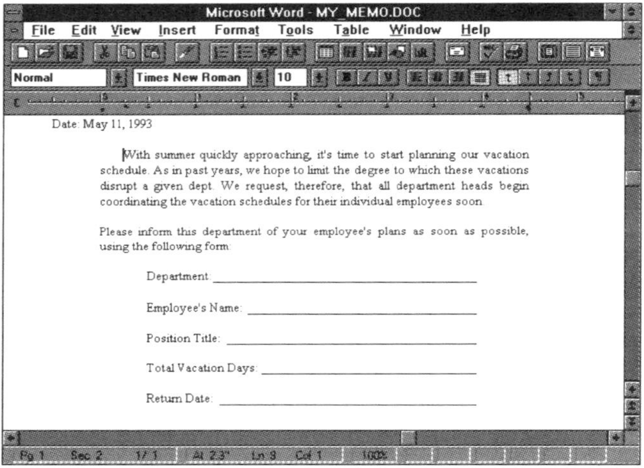

Figure 21.1   The first-line marker lets you manually indent paragraphs.

2. Point to the first-line indent marker, the top arrow pointing to the right immediately below **0** on the Ruler bar.
3. Hold down the left mouse button.
4. Drag the first-line indent marker to the right 1/4", until it's approximately halfway between **0** and the first tab marker.
5. Release the left mouse button.

Your screen should now resemble Figure 21.1, which shows the first line indented 1/4", relative to the rest of the paragraph.

To indent multiple paragraphs:

1. Use the first-line indent marker to return the first paragraph to its previous indentation.

2. Double click on the selection bar immediately to the left of the first paragraph.
3. Hold down the **Shift** key and double click on the selection bar immediately to the left of the second paragraph.
4. Point to the first-line indent marker.
5. Hold down the left mouse button.
6. This time, drag the first-line indent marker to the left approximately 1/2" on the ruler bar.
7. Release the left mouse button.

Your screen should now resemble Figure 21.2, which shows both paragraphs "outdented" half an inch so that they line up with the **Date** line at the top of the memo.

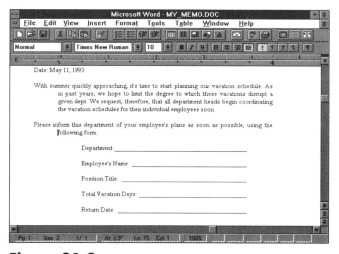

Figure 21.2 It's easy to indent multiple paragraphs.

Setting and Changing Line Spacing

The topic covered in this lesson—line spacing—is another relatively simple but important concept. As the name implies, line spacing determines the amount of space that appears between printed lines in a document.

When it comes to line spacing, Word for Windows possesses major advantages over earlier writing methods—using a typewriter or pen and paper. Traditionally, you were limited to placing a single or double space between lines. Word for Windows allows for much greater flexibility.

Setting Paragraph Line Spacing

By default, Word for Windows automatically adjusts line spacing based on the size of the letters being printed. This default setting, however, is easy to change.

1. Double click on the selection bar immediately to the left of the first paragraph.

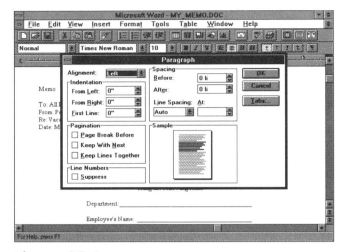

Figure 22.1 The Paragraph dialog box is used for many purposes.

2. Select **Format** from the Word for Windows Menu bar.
3. Select the **Paragraph** option.

This displays the Paragraph dialog box, shown in Figure 22.1, which we used in Lesson 20 to modify alignment. This time, we'll use it to adjust line spacing for the selected paragraph.

To select a new line spacing:

1. Click on the down arrow to the right of the **Line Spacing** field to display the drop-down box list.
2. Click on **1.5 Lines**. (Notice that the representative page in the **Sample** window changes to reflect your new choice.)
3. Click on **OK**.

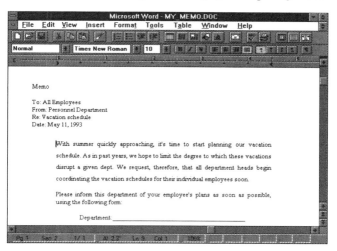

Figure 22.2   Word for Windows automatically adjusts the selected paragraph to the new line spacing.

Your screen should now resemble Figure 22.2, which shows the line spacing of the first paragraph adjusted to 1.5 lines; that is, 1.5 times the size of capital letters in the current typeface.

Before we move on to the next section, repeat the previous steps to change the line spacing of the first paragraph back to the **Auto** setting.

◆ *Lesson* ◆

23
Using Fonts

Once you've established the basic design of a document—margin settings, alignment, line spacing, and so forth—Word for Windows provides a number of ways to enhance its final appearance. One of the more useful of these is the ability to modify the size and appearance of selected text using a variety of typefaces available in Word for Windows.

What Are Typefaces?

Stated simply, a specific typeface is defined by a combination of two attributes:

- the way in which its letters are designed, called the font
- the size of those letters, also called their point size

Word for Windows profits greatly from Windows WYSIWYG (remember, this stands for what-you-see-is-what-you-get) design, especially when it comes to letting you select and preview a typeface. To see what I mean:

1. Click on the selection bar immediately to the left of the word **Memo** at the beginning of our sample document.

2. Select **Format** from the Word for Windows Menu bar.

3. Select the **Character** option.

This displays the Character dialog box shown in Figure 23.1, from which you specify typeface attributes—character design, size, and some additional properties—for selected text.

We'll begin by selecting a new font for the word "Memo."

Click on the down arrow to the right of **Font** field.

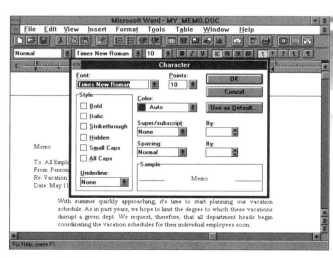

Figure 23.1 The Character dialog box

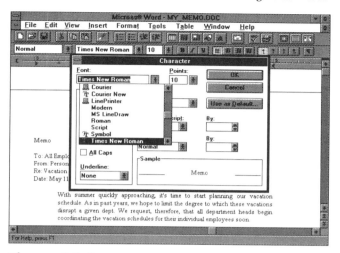

Figure 23.2 Word for Windows provides a variety of fonts for your documents.

This displays a drop-down list box containing the various fonts available to Word for Windows. (See Figure 23.2.) Before moving on, let's examine the contents of this box more closely. Doing so will help you use fonts effectively.

Understanding Font Types

Notice the various symbols to the left of the font names listed in Figure 23.2. These symbols indicate the kind of font a particular selection is. Options include:

- The double "TT" indicates a Windows True Type scalable font. Times New Roman, the currently active font, is an example of a True Type font. These fonts, new to Windows 3.1, use a single file to print typefaces at virtually any point size. Scalable fonts give you much greater control over the appearance of a document.

- Other listed fonts are nonscalable; that is, they are available only in specific, predefined point sizes.
- Finally, Windows WYSIWYG design has created a lucrative market for third-party fonts, add-in packages that, once installed in your Windows environment, make even more typefaces available for your Word for Windows documents. One of the most popular is the Adobe Type Manager.

Selecting a Font

With this admittedly brief explanation of fonts out of the way, let's select a new one for the Memo line in our sample document.

1. Use the scroll bar to display the **Arial** option.
2. Click on **Arial**. (Notice that the representative word in the **Sample** window changes to reflect your new choice.)
3. Click on the down arrow to the right of **Points** field to display a drop-down list box showing the point sizes available for the Arial font.
4. Select **18**.
5. Click on **OK**.

Your screen should now resemble Figure 23.3. Notice that the word "Memo" has changed to the new typeface.

We'll be making additional modifications to the fonts in this and other sections of our memo in the

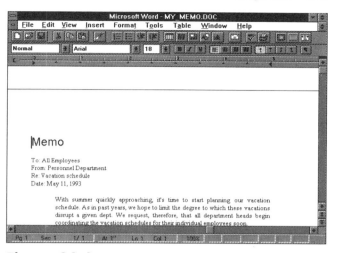

Figure 23.3 Windows WYSIWYG display reflects your changes.

next lesson. Before moving on, however, let's discuss briefly some general guidelines to help you use fonts wisely.

Choosing Fonts for Your Document

Professional typesetters spend years learning how to create attractive documents. Selecting just the right number and kinds of typefaces to create a truly attractive finished product is as much an art as it is a science. With all of the options available in Word for Windows, it's easy for someone inexperienced in the "ins-and-outs" of professional typesetting to overdo it. Following are some simple guidelines to help you avoid this pitfall, when selecting typefaces for your documents:

1. Whenever possible, limit the number of fonts on a single page to two—three at the most. For emphasis and appearance, when necessary, modify point size and other attributes—boldface, italics, and so forth (discussed in the next lesson).
2. A good rule of thumb is to pick one serif and one sans serif font (defined below), usually used for body text and headline text, respectively.

The terms serif and sans serif apply to how the individual letters within a font are designed. Generally speaking, serif fonts are more traditional than sans serif fonts. They are distinguished by the short lines extending from the upper and lower ends of the strokes of letters. Sans serif fonts do not have these extensions; they are considered more modern in design. The Times New Roman font used for the majority of our memo is an example of a serif font. The Arial font we selected for the first line of our sample memo is an example of a sans serif font.

Serif and sans serif fonts complement one another well, when they appear on the same page. Hence, rule 2, above. The overriding factor to keep in mind when mixing and matching typefaces is to design your documents to inform, not impress. Don't get too fancy. Remember, clutter rarely communicates.

◆ *Lesson* ◆

24

Changing Font Attributes

Given our discussion at the end of the previous lesson, you may be wondering how it's possible to create truly stunning documents using only two fonts—the recommended number. The answer to this question lies in Word for Windows ability to enhance the appearance of selected text with a variety of font attributes: boldface, italics, underlining, and so forth.

More Font-astic Changes

Before getting into these specific topics, however, let's use the Word for Windows Toolbar, rather than the Character dialog box, to modify quickly the fonts used in several other sections of our sample memo. We're going to move quickly here, so pay attention.

1. Point to the selection bar to the left of the "To:" line, directly below "Memo" in our sample document.
2. Hold down the left mouse button.

3. Drag the mouse pointer down the screen until all four lines of the memo introduction are highlighted.

4. Release the left mouse button.

5. Point to the down arrow just to the right of the number **10** in the Toolbar.

6. Click the left mouse button to display a drop-down list box containing the available font sizes for the Times New Roman font.

7. Click on **12**.

8. Use the scroll bar to display the five lines requesting specific information about employee vacation time. (**Department, Employee's Name**, etc.)

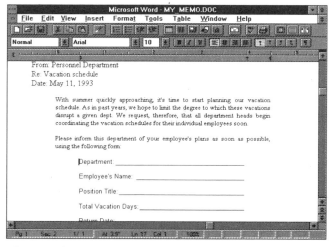

Figure 24.1 You can use the Toolbar to adjust fonts.

9. Use the selection bar to highlight these five lines.

10. Point to the down arrow just to the right of the font listing (**Times New Roman**) in the Toolbar.

11. Click the left mouse button to display a drop-down list box containing the available fonts.

12. Click on **Arial**.

When you've finished the previous steps, your screen should resemble Figure 24.1. Notice that a new typeface has been assigned to the specified lines. As this exercise demonstrates, it's easy to use the Toolbar to adjust fonts and font sizes. Next, let's begin really spiffing up our memo.

Selecting Font Attributes

Once again, we're going to move quickly. In the following exercise, however, we're going to use various Toolbar options to add font attributes to selected sections of our sample document.

1. Use the scroll bars to display the first line of the memo.

2. Point to the selection bar to the left of this line.

3. Click on the **Centered** alignment button (the second alignment button from the left) in the Word for Windows Toolbar.

4. Click on the **Underline** button (a stylized u) in the Toolbar.

5. Click on the **Boldface** button (a stylized **B**) in the Toolbar.

6. Use the scroll bar to display the five lines requesting specific information about employee vacation time. (**Department, Employee's Name**, etc.)

7. Use the selection bar to highlight these five lines.

8. Click on the **Boldface** button in the Toolbar.

9. Use the mouse to highlight the phrase "as soon as possible" in the line preceding the lines you just modified.

10. Click on the **Italics** button (a stylized **I**) in the Toolbar.

11. Use the scroll bar to display the portion of the sample memo shown in Figure 24.2.

Memo

To: All Employees
From: Personnel Department
Re: Vacation schedule
Date: May 11, 1993

With summer quickly approaching, it's time to start planning our vacation schedule. As in past years, we hope to limit the degree to which these vacations disrupt a given dept. We request, therefore, that all department heads begin coordinating the vacation schedules for their individual employees soon.

Please inform this department of your employee's plans *as soon as possible*, using the following form:

Department: _____

Employee's Name: _____

Figure 24.2   A few mouse clicks transform a bland memo into an attractive and effective document.

To see the results of the previous exercise, print out the memo in its current form, using procedures outlined in Lesson 13. This document provides a dramatic example of the formatting capabilities of Word for Windows. And we're not finished yet. In the next lesson we'll examine how to create formatted lists quickly in Word for Windows.

25

Creating Bulleted and Numbered Lists

Word for Windows makes it easy to format information contained in a document as bulleted or numbered lists. As has been the case so often in previous exercises, doing so is a simple point-and-click procedure.

Creating Bulleted Lists

Bulleted lists are useful for highlighting important information presented as a series of short items or sentences, as you've seen throughout this book. In our sample memo, for example, it might make sense to convert the five lines used to record vacation information into a bulleted list. To do so:

1. Use the scroll bar to display the five blank lines for specific information about employee vacation time. (**Department, Employee's Name**, etc.)
2. Use the selection bar to highlight these five lines.

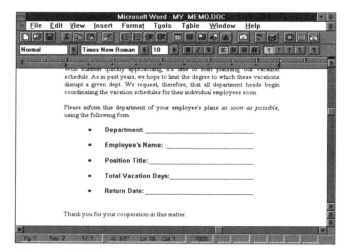

Figure 25.1 Bulleted lists add emphasis to your documents.

3. Point to the **Bulleted List** Toolbar button—a stylized bulleted list immediately below the **Format** option on the Word for Windows Menu bar.

4. Click the left mouse button.

Word for Windows converts the selected lines into a bulleted list, as shown in Figure 25.1. How's that for easy?

Specifying a Different Bullet Symbol

As Figure 25.1 illustrates, the initial bullet symbol is a small circle. If desired, you can change this.

1. With the same five lines highlighted, select **Tools** from the Word for Windows Menu bar.

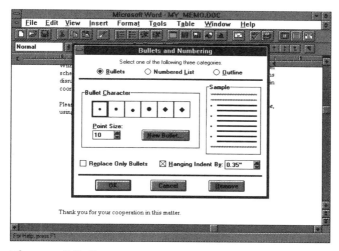

Figure 25.2 The Bullets and Numbering option box

2. Select the **Bullets and Numbering** option, which displays the dialog box shown in Figure 25.2 where you choose the formatting you want applied to selected text.

3. The **Bullet Character** window displays several default symbols available for a Word for Windows bulleted list. If you don't like any of these, the **New Bullet** command button can be used to select from a variety of other symbols.

4. Click on the **New Bullet** command button, which displays the **Symbol** dialog box shown in Figure 25.3. Notice that the box containing the current bullet symbol is highlighted.

5. To select a different bullet symbol, click on the heart symbol in the third row from the bottom.

6. Click on **OK**.

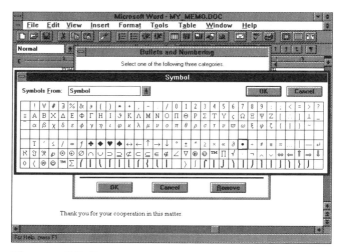

Figure 25.3 You can choose from a variety of bullet symbols.

7. When the Bullets and Numbering dialog box reappears, click on **OK**. Word for Windows changes the bullet symbol preceding the five information lines in our sample memo to hearts.

Creating a Numbered List

Hearts are nice, but hardly appropriate for an "official" business memo. A better approach would be a numbered list, so let's create one.

1. With the five information lines highlighted, point to the **Numbered List** Toolbar button—a stylized numbered list just to the left of the Bulleted List button.
2. Click the left mouse button.

3. When Word for Windows displays a prompt box asking you to verify the current operation, click on **Yes**.

Word for Windows converts the selected lines into a numbered list, as shown in Figure 25.4. That was almost as easy as creating the initial bulleted list, wasn't it?

Our sample memo has really started to take shape over the past few lessons. And all you've done is click the mouse button a few times. In the next lesson, you'll discover that expanding this one-page memo into a two-page document is an equally easy procedure.

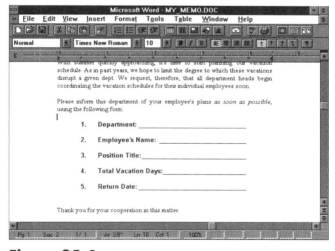

Figure 25.4 It's also easy to create numbered lists in a Word for Windows document.

26

Managing Page Breaks in a Document

Next we'll make our sample memo a little easier to use for the people who receive it. Although we've already included a form on which they can record vacation information, it would be more convenient still if this form were isolated on a single page. They could then photocopy that page and distribute it to their employees. A simple page break will accomplish this.

Inserting Page Breaks

Inserting a page break into a document forces Word for Windows to print any text following the page break on a new sheet of paper. Making the following changes to our sample memo will demonstrate how this works.

1. Replace the phrase "the following form:" with **the form on the following page. Feel free to copy this form, as necessary, for the employees of your department.**
2. Press **Enter**.

3. Select **Insert** from the Word for Windows Menu bar.

4. Select the **Break** option.

5. At the Break dialog box, activate the **Page Break** button, if necessary.

6. Click on **OK**.

Your screen should now resemble Figure 26.1, which shows the numbered list designed to record vacation information on a page by itself. Notice that the status bar identifies this as a second page in our sample memo (**Pg 2**).

A few more steps, and we're almost finished. Given that all of these operations involve procedures we've

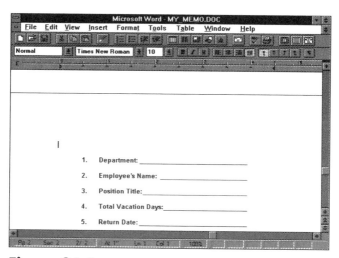

Figure 26.1 Page breaks help you control the overall structure of your document.

covered previously, I'm just going to list them quickly. If you're unsure how to perform a particular step, review the appropriate lesson.

1. Type **1992 VACATION SCHEDULES**.
2. Press **Enter**.
3. Use the selection bar to highlight this new line.
4. Choose **Arial** from the drop-down Fonts box list in the Ribbon bar.
5. Choose **18** from the drop-down Point Size box list in the ribbon bar.
6. Click on the **Center** alignment button in the Ribbon bar.
7. Click on the **Boldface** button in the Ribbon bar.
8. Click on the **Underline** button in the Ribbon bar.
9. Delete the final line of text in the sample memo that currently reads: "Thank you for your cooperation in this matter."

Your screen should now resemble Figure 26.2, which shows our vacation questionnaire page formatted to its final appearance. Pretty impressive, isn't it?

Controlling Widows and Orphans

Page breaks also can be used to help prevent widows and orphans. The Word for Windows default is set to eliminate widows and orphans by automatically inserting a page break before or after the offending line of text, as appropriate. At your discretion, however, you can change this default setting. To do so:

1. Select **Tools** from the Menu bar.

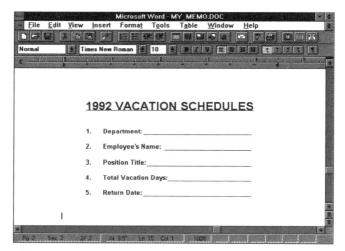

Figure 26.2   A page break and some additional formatting creates an isolated, attractive looking questionnaire.

2. Select the **Options** option.
3. Click on the **Print** icon to the left of the Options dialog box.

This displays the dialog box shown in Figure 26.3. Clicking on the check box to the left of **Widow/Orphan Control** will turn off automatic page breaks for widows and orphans when you print the current document. However, we won't do this. So for now:

Click on the **Cancel** command button.

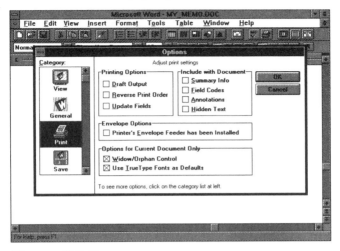

Figure 26.3 Use the Tools/Options dialog box to turn off Word for Windows automatic widow/orphan control.

Tip

Manually inserted page breaks override Word for Windows automatic widow/orphan control. Manual page breaks provide a way to permit a widow or an orphan appearing in a printout, if necessary, without turning off automatic page formatting for the entire document. You can add a manual page break either by choosing the Insert Break menu option, selecting the Page Break radio button, and clicking on OK.

27

Inserting Headers, Footers, and Page Numbers

As your Word for Windows documents get longer, the need to organize them increases. Items such as headers, footers, and page numbering can help a reader navigate a large document. Although we only recently expanded our sample memo to two pages in length, we can use it to demonstrate the steps involved in creating these convenient features.

Accessing the Headers/Footers Dialog Box

A header or footer is descriptive text that is printed at the top or bottom of document pages, respectively. The typical book, for example, generally includes a header containing the book's title and, in many cases, either the author's name or title of the current chapter. The footer of a book generally contains page numbers.

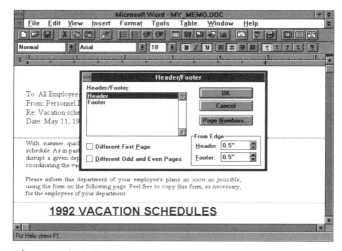

Figure 27.1   The Header/Footer dialog box

Word for Windows allows you to insert similar items in your documents.

1. Select **View** from the Word for Windows Menu bar.
2. Select the **Normal** option. (You must be in Normal view to create a header or footer.)
3. Select **View** from the Word for Windows Menu bar.
4. Select the **Header/Footer** option.

This displays the Header/Footer dialog box shown in Figure 27.1. Don't let the relatively plain appearance of this dialog box fool you. It gives you amazing control over the headers and footers that are included with your documents.

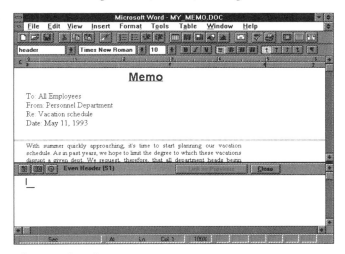

Figure 27.2   You can define different headers and footers for odd and even numbered pages.

Defining a Header

We're going to define a different header for each page of our sample memo. To do this:

1. Click on the check box for **Different Odd and Even Pages**.
2. Click on **OK**.

Word for Windows displays the Even Header input window shown in Figure 27.2. Use this window to define the contents of the headers you want to appear on even-numbered pages.

1. Press **Tab** to center this header.
2. Type **FOR: ALL DEPARTMENT HEADS**.

3. Click on **Close**.
4. Select **View** from the Word for Windows Menu bar.
5. Select the **Header/Footer** option.
6. Click on **Odd Header**.
7. Click on **OK**.
8. When the Odd Header window appears, press **Tab** to center this header.
9. Type **VACATION MEMO**.
10. Click on **Close**.
11. Select **View** from the Word for Windows Menu bar.
12. Select the **Header/Footer** option.
13. Click on **Even Footer**.
14. Click on **OK**.
15. When the Even Footer window appears, click on the Page Number icon (**#**).
16. Select **View** from the Word for Windows Menu bar.
17. Select the **Page Layout** option.
18. Select **File** from the Word for Windows Menu bar.
19. Select the **Print Preview**.

Your screen should now resemble Figure 27.3, which shows the second page of our sample memo as it will appear when printed. Use the **Margins** option as outlined in Lesson 12 to center the information on this page.

After centering this form, try the following:

1. Click on **Margins** to remove the margin lines.
2. Click on **Two Pages**.

3. Use the **PgUp** and **PgDn** keys to view the two pages of our sample memo.

4. When you're finished, select **Close** to return to the main Word for Windows display.

This ends the creation and formatting of our sample memo. Go ahead and print it out, if you want to, as a reward for all your efforts over the previous lessons. But just because we've completed this document, doesn't mean we're finished with Word for Windows. In the next lesson we'll use a longer file to examine how Word for Windows lets you format documents with multiple columns.

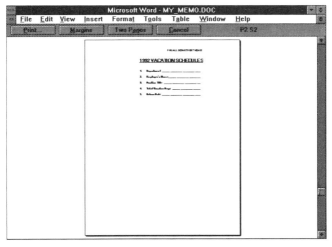

Figure 27.3 Word for Windows automatically incorporates headers and footers into your printed pages.

◆ *Lesson* ◆

28

Working with Columns

Many documents rely on multiple columns to be effective. These include newsletters, reports, and brochures, to name but three kinds of documents often designed around a multicolumn format. In this, our final "hands-on" lesson, we'll examine the Word for Windows commands used to break a page of text into multiple columns.

First, however, let's close the sample memo that has served us so well to this point.

1. Select **File** from the Menu bar.
2. Select **Close**.
3. When Word for Windows asks if you want to save your changes, select **Yes**.

This clears the Word for Windows display so that you can open another document. Let's do this now, using a sample document shipped with Word for Windows.

1. Select **File** from the Menu bar.
2. Select **Open**.

3. Double-click on **winword.cbt** in the Directories window.

4. Double-click on **busrep.doc** in the File Name window.

This loads a marketing plan for FilmWatch, a division of an imaginary company called Trey Research. This sample document contains enough text to experiment with multiple columns. Before doing so, however, let's save this document with a new name to preserve the original for use with Word for Windows on-line training course.

1. Select **File** from the Word for Windows Menu bar.

2. Select **Save As**.

3. Type **column.doc** in the File Name text box.

4. Click on **OK**.

5. At the Summary Info dialog box, click on **OK**.

Selecting a Multicolumn Format

Now that we have a new document to work with, we can begin examining how to divide a document into multiple columns.

Click on the **Text Columns** button in the Word for Windows Toolbar, the stylized two-column button directly below the Table option on the Word for Windows Menu bar.

This displays the Text Columns selection box shown in Figure 28.1, which is used to specify the number of

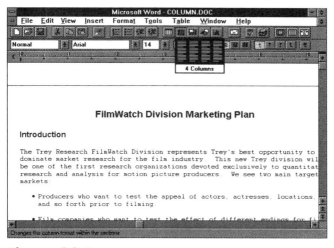

Figure 28.1   The Text Columns selection box

columns into which you want to divide the current document.

To specify a two-column format:

1. Point to the left-most column in the Text Columns selection box.
2. Hold down the left mouse button.
3. Drag your mouse to the right until two columns are highlighted.
4. Release the left mouse button.

Your screen should now resemble Figure 28.2, which does *not* look like a two-column format, does it? Instead, it looks like Word for Windows only moved the

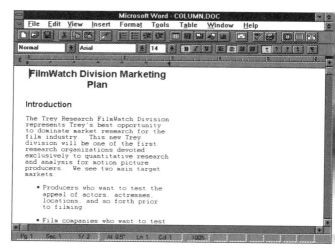

Figure 28.2   Word for Windows rearranges your text after you select a two-column format.

right margin in several inches. But trust me, this isn't the case, as you'll see in a few seconds.

Displaying a Columnar Layout

To see the actual results of the previous exercise:

1. Select **View** from the Word for Windows Menu bar.
2. Select the **Page Layout** option.

Now the screen is redrawn to display two columns of text, as shown in Figure 28.3. The reason? Word for Windows is using its Page Layout view to present a true WYSIWYG display of multicolumn text.

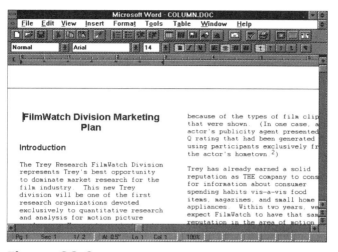

Figure 28.3 You must use the Page Layout view to display multiple columns of text.

Mixing Single and Multiple Columns on a Page

Of course, the two columns currently displayed are primitive, to say the least. It would look much better if the title of this article remained in a single column, running all the way across the page. A few mouse clicks is all it will take.

1. Place the insertion point before the word **Introduction**.
2. Select **Insert** from the Word for Windows Menu bar.
3. Select the **Break** option.
4. Turn on the **Continuous** option.

5. Click on **OK**.
6. Place the insertion point before the title (FilmWatch Division Marketing Plan).
7. Click on the **Text Columns** button in the Word for Windows Toolbar.
8. Point to the left-most column in the Text Columns selection box.
9. Hold down the left mouse button.
10. With only one column highlighted, release the left mouse button.

This returns the title to a single-column format, while retaining the multicolumn format previously applied to the body of the file (see Figure 28.4). As this example demonstrates, different columnar formats can

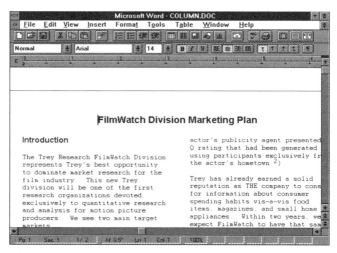

Figure 28.4 Dividing a document into sections lets you "mix-and-match" column layouts.

be applied to separate sections of the same Word for Windows document.

Save the reformatted marketing plan so that you'll be able to come back to it later and experiment further with multicolumn layouts. But first, stick around for the next and final lesson. In it, we'll tie up our discussion of Word for Windows features by looking at some of the program's more advanced features.

Being Creative with Word for Windows

We've covered an amazing number of Word for Windows features in the previous 28 lessons, and yet we've barely scratched the surface. Some of the more impressive capabilities of this robust program that remain unexamined include:

- indexes and tables of contents
- table generation
- the ability to include graphics in documents
- the creation and use of style sheets
- automating repetitive operations with macros and wizards
- incorporating calculations in a document
- automatic line numbering
- automatic hyphenation
- sorting columnar data
- envelope printing and mail merge
- customizing the Toolbar

And the list goes on. To be honest, a complete litany of Word for Windows features would fill this book.

Had I tried to cover everything, we would not have been able to incorporate the "hands-on" lessons, which were designed primarily to help you feel comfortable using the basic text editing and document formatting features of Word for Windows. In the few pages we have left, therefore, let's take a quick glance at some of the Word for Windows operations not discussed in the body of this book.

Mail Merge

Figure 29.1 shows a sample letter included in the Word for Windows CBT (computer-based training) course, an on-line tutorial that Setup transferred to your hard disk in Lesson 2.

Notice the generic terms enclosed in double brackets (<< >>) at the beginning of this letter (name, address, city, and so forth). They allow you to take information stored in an external file—a database, for example—and merge it into your document at print time. One popular use for Mail Merge is mass mailings, where a personalized copy of the same letter is sent to several individuals. Used wisely, Mail Merge can be an effective marketing technique.

Printing Envelopes

Figure 29.2 shows the Create Envelope dialog box. Word for Windows uses information about your system printer that's already recorded in the Windows environment to fully automate the printing of mailing and return addresses on an envelope. Anyone who's ever tried to use embedded control codes to prepare an

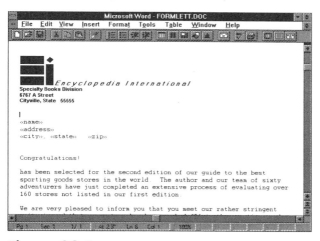

Figure 29.1 Mail Merge lets you personalize mass mailings.

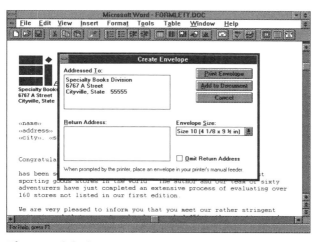

Figure 29.2 Word for Windows automates the printing of envelopes.

envelope for mailing will truly appreciate this Word for Windows feature.

Setting the Table

Figure 29.3 shows a table within a document. This figure also illustrates several other Word for Windows features. Notice that I've highlighted one column of figures within this table. Using various Word for Windows commands, I could now perform a number of operations on the information this table contains. These include:

- Sorting the table in ascending or descending order, based on the contents of the selected column of data.

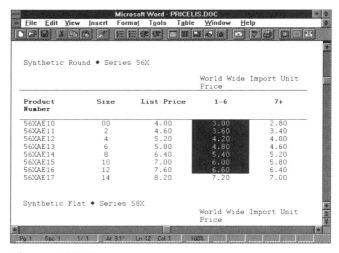

Figure 29.3   Word for Windows lets you create and manipulate tables of information.

- Perform mathematical calculations on selected data and incorporate the results in the table or another section of a document.
- Insert, delete, and rearrange columns and rows within a table.
- Modify the size of rows and columns to create a more attractive table.

Getting Graphic

Figure 29.4 illustrates what is perhaps one of Word for Windows most impressive features: the ability to combine text and graphics on a single page. It is this capability, more than any other, that allows Word for

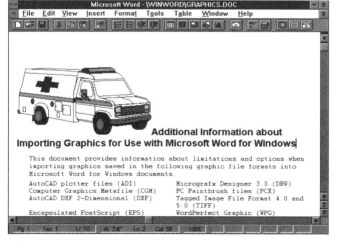

Figure 29.4 Word for Windows lets you mix words and pictures in your documents.

Windows to straddle the fence between traditional word processing and desktop publishing.

Word for Windows will import graphics created with a number of popular application programs. These include:

- DrawPerfect
- PC Paintbrush
- Lotus 1-2-3
- AutoCAD
- Micrographx Designer

In addition to these specific applications, Word for Windows can work with graphic images stored in a variety of file formats, regardless of the program used to create them. These include:

- Windows Metafile format (WMF files)
- Encapsulated PostScript format (EPS files)
- Tagged Image File Format (TIFF or TIF files)
- Hewlett-Packard Graphic Language format (HGL files)
- Windows Bitmaps (BMP files)
- PC Paintbrush format (PCX files)
- Lotus Freelance format (PIC files)
- WordPerfect graphics format (WPG files)

Built-in Graphics Tools

Word for Windows itself contains two valuable tools for adding visual panache to your documents:

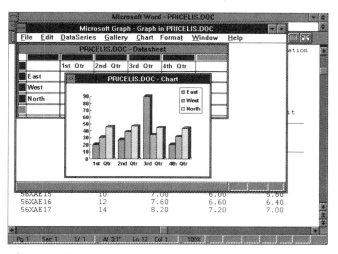

Figure 29.5 Microsoft Graph can be used to create graphs and charts.

Microsoft Graph and Microsoft Chart. Figure 29.5 shows a bar chart created with Microsoft Graph, based on the column of figures highlighted in Figure 29.3. Once a graph or chart exists, it's easy to insert it into your document at a specified location.

A second Word for Windows utility, Microsoft Draw, lets you design and create your own graphic images, which can then be imported into a document. Graphics created with Draw can include geometric shapes, text and freehand drawings, among other items. Figure 29.6 shows a sample (and admittedly primitive) graphic image created with Microsoft Draw.

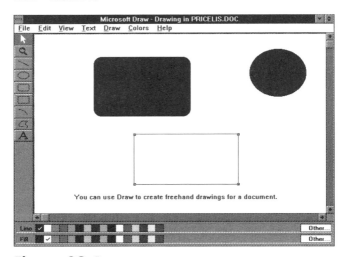

Figure 29.6 Microsoft Draw can be used to create freehand drawings.

Conclusion

The underlying message in this lesson is a simple one: Word for Windows provides a wealth of features, utilities, and other tools that, once mastered, will allow you to produce truly stunning printed documents.

Few people would deny that Johann Guttenberg's invention of movable type in the fifteenth century forever altered history. Suddenly, knowledge and information were easily disseminated, and become readily accessible to all humanity, not just the intellectually elite. Word for Windows places similar power, quite literally, at your fingertips. Obviously, it will require some time and effort to learn all the "ins and outs" of Word for Windows, to master all the features available in this amazingly powerful program. In the end, however, this effort will be well rewarded.

The various exercises in this book have introduced you to the basic Word for Windows commands and procedures. Now it's time to begin experimenting on your own. Have fun.

Epilogue
Where to Go From Here

As mentioned several times throughout this book, my main goal here was to help you master the basics commands and procedures in Word for Windows. Consider this a foundation on which you can now build true expertise. So, where do you go from here?

A good place to start would be with one of Word for Windows on-line computer-based tutorials, or CBTs. Two of them are available:

- Getting Started
- Learning Word

Either tutorial can be run by selecting the appropriate option in the pull-down **Help** menu.

After that, you may want to read some of the following books. They contain more comprehensive information about either the Windows GUI or Word for Windows itself: *Peter Norton's User's Guide to Windows 3.1*, by Peter Norton and Peter Kent; *Word for Windows Companion*, by Mark W. Crane.

Index